JUDIE HAYNES

Getting Started with English Language Learners

How Educators Can Meet the Challenge

ASCD

Alexandria, Virginia USA

ASCD®

1703 N. Beauregard St. • Alexandria, VA 22311-1714 USA
Phone: 800-933-2723 or 703-578-9600 • Fax: 703-575-5400
Web site: www.ascd.org • E-mail: member@ascd.org
Author guidelines: www.ascd.org/write

Gene R. Carter, *Executive Director*; Nancy Modrak, *Director of Publishing*; Julie Houtz, *Director of Book Editing & Production*; Leah Lakins, *Project Manager*; Greer Beeken, *Graphic Designer*; Barton Matheson Willse & Worthington, *Desktop Publishing*; Dina Murray Seamon, *Production Specialist/Team Lead*

Portions of this book first appeared on the author's Web site, http://www.everythingesl.net.

All Web links in this book are correct as of the publication date below but may have become inactive or otherwise modified since that time. If you notice a deactivated or changed link, please e-mail books@ascd.org with the words "Link Update" in the subject line. In your message, please specify the Web link, the book title, and the page number on which the link appears.

PAPERBACK ISBN: 978-1-4166-0519-5   ASCD product #106048   s02/07
Also available as an e-book through ebrary, netLibrary, and many online booksellers (see Books in Print for the ISBNs).

Quantity discounts for the paperback edition only: 10–49 copies, 10%; 50+ copies, 15%; for 1,000 or more copies, call 800-933-2723, ext. 5634, or 703-575-5634. For desk copies: member@ascd.org.

Library of Congress Cataloging-in-Publication Data

Haynes, Judie.
    Getting started with English language learners : how educators can meet the challenge / Judie Haynes.
        p. cm.
    Includes bibliographical references and index.
    ISBN-13: 978-1-4166-0519-5 (pbk. : alk. paper)
    ISBN-10: 1-4166-0519-3 (pbk. : alk. paper)
    1. Linguistic minorities—Education (Elementary)—United States.   2. Children of immigrants—Education (Elementary)—United States.   3. English language—Study and teaching (Elementary)—United States—Foreign speakers.   I. Title.

    LC3725.H39 2007
    428.2'4—dc22

                                                                  2006033208

18 17 16 15 14 13 12 11 10   3 4 5 6 7 8 9 10 11 12

Getting Started with | English Language Learners

How Educators Can Meet the Challenge

Acknowledgments

After 26 years of teaching, I still approach each day with enthusiasm. This is largely due to the caring and dedicated professionals whom I have worked with over the years at River Edge Schools in River Edge, New Jersey. Many of these outstanding colleagues have contributed their expertise to this book in the form of the many classroom scenarios. Thanks to these friends: Nancy Appert, Janet Arena, Peggy Charbonnel, Pat Wondra, Susan Boucher, Christine Murphy, Sue Meldonian, Carolyn Brush, Patrice Pintarelli, Christine Gorman, Vanessa Hernandez, Sandy Lautz, Julie Mahoney, Joann Frechette, JoAnn Jennings, Ginny Millard, Nancy Du Bois, and Denise Heitman.

A very special acknowledgment to Monica Schnee for writing the foreword to this book and for all of her expertise and encouragement. I would also like to also thank Dr. Grisel Lopez-Diaz for editing the first draft and for her helpful suggestions.

Thanks to my caring family for their support: my husband Joe, my daughter and son-in-law Jennifer and Brian Clark, grandchildren Devin and Owen, and sons Joe and Chas Haynes. I want to especially acknowledge Chas, who designed and continues to improve my Web site, everythingESL.net, for me.

I'd also like to thank ASCD acquisitions editor Carolyn Pool and associate editor Leah Lakins for their hard work and patience.

Foreword

By Monica Schnee

As the number of English language learners continues to grow in our classrooms, *Getting Started with English Language Learners* will prove to be a valuable resource for administrators and practitioners. Approximately 5 million English language learners were enrolled in our public schools during the 2003–2004 school year. This figure represents 10 percent of the total school population according to a report to the Congressional Requesters by the U.S. Government Accountability Office in July 2006. Because of these numbers and the demands placed by the No Child Left Behind Act (NCLB) of 2002, teachers and administrators are facing a tremendous challenge to teach and assess this diverse population.

Title III of NCLB addresses English language learners in particular. Because states are required to set goals that demonstrate adequate yearly progress (AYP), states must develop English language proficiency standards that are aligned with each state's academic content standards. All English language learners, from kindergarten to 12th grade, must demonstrate adequate yearly progress, regardless of whether these students are required to take standardized tests for assessment.

Many English language learners are placed in classrooms where teachers are very knowledgeable about their subject matter, yet have limited experience working with non-English-speaking students. Judie Haynes clearly and concisely explains to educators who are unfamiliar with second-language acquisition how students acquire a second language. She illustrates different scenarios from her own experiences and provides specific and useful strategies that teachers can easily implement in their classrooms.

Getting Started with English Language Learners addresses the challenges that administrators, supervisors, and teachers are faced with every day. Judie Haynes shares her experience and knowledge from years of helping English language learners understand not only English and academic content but also the customs, history, and mores of United States culture that help students become active participants in their schools and communities. As you read this book, you will discover new ways of working with English language learners and, in many cases, you will validate what you are already practicing in your classroom.

Getting Started with English Language Learners is written in a friendly and accessible way and can be used by supervisors to provide staff development. The book is also ideal for discussion with faculty members to help them learn and generate new ways to improve the performance of English language learners. Judie has successfully put together a "mini second-language acquisition handbook" for staff members who are struggling to develop effective strategies to help ELLs meet the demands set by NCLB and its requirements. She provides educators with an engaging, hands-on, practical resource that can be used by all professionals who are working with English language learners. Classroom teachers and content-area teachers will find a menu of different strategies and techniques that can be used with all learners, whether students are native English speakers or English language learners.

There is no better time for *Getting Started with English Language Learners*. It is a simple, clear, how-to guide that addresses some of the most pressing issues in our schools today. As a professional working in this field, I feel that this book should become a staple in every administrator's office and in every teacher's library. Thank you, Judie, for sharing your invaluable experience.

Introduction

Getting Started with English Language Learners: How Educators Can Meet the Challenge is written for teachers, administrators, board of education members, and teacher trainers in the United States who are responsible for educating the growing number of English language learners (ELLs) in our public schools. The book's aim is to help you provide an effective learning environment for ELLs.

This book is based on my personal experience and passionate involvement in the field of English language education over the past 26 years. It is not meant to be a research document but a practical resource to help educators who are not specialists in the field of English as a Second Language (ESL) understand the needs of English language learners. I wish also to help administrators and board members implement programs to help English language learners reach the learning level of their native English-speaking classmates. Throughout the book I have provided scenarios of actual classrooms and real students both in my own school and in the schools of my colleagues throughout the United States.

Information about instructing English language learners has become vital over the past few years as school districts wrestle with the guidelines mandated by No Child Left Behind (NCLB). NCLB contains significant changes regarding federal policies that directly affect mainstream classroom teachers and individual school districts in the following areas:

• All English language learners must be tested at least once a year using an English proficiency test. They are no longer exempt from statewide accountability.

• Students who have been in U.S. schools for three consecutive years and have been tested in their native language must be tested in English for reading and language arts. They are required to meet the same standards as their native English-speaking peers and demonstrate adequate yearly progress (AYP).

• Standards for English language proficiency need to be tied to core curriculum content standards.

• In the past, English proficiency tests for ELLs assessed basic communication skills such as listening, speaking, reading, and writing. Now subject-area academic skills must also be tested.

These guidelines place the classroom teacher and the school districts on center stage. Teachers are obliged to ensure that teaching strategies in their classrooms are aligned with English language proficiency standards. These standards make it imperative for mainstream teachers to learn about the theories and teaching strategies that have been used successfully to teach ELLs.

The first three chapters cover essential concepts to help you understand how children learn a second language. I implore you not to skip these chapters because they contain crucial knowledge for educators who are making decisions about English language learners in their classrooms, schools, and school districts. In these first chapters I also discuss how long it takes ELLs to learn English and review the stages of second-language acquisition. In Chapters 4, 5, and 6, I focus on practical strategies for teaching newcomers and address how to differentiate instruction for students who are not ready to undertake grade-level work. I also discuss what approaches skilled teachers use to provide the best possible education for ELLs.

The last chapter gives a brief overview of the different types of programs used in the United States. This is not meant to be a definitive review of all programs, but it is a short synopsis of popular alternatives that provide effective instruction for English language learners.

1

Key Concepts of Second-Language Acquisition

Many popular beliefs about second-language acquisition are per-petuated in our society. The following statements are related to six key concepts of second-language acquisition. Check the ones you think are true.

☐ My newcomer should be referred to the child study team. He is often disruptive in the classroom and kicks and hits other children. There is something wrong with him aside from not knowing the language.

☐ The more time students spend soaking up English in the mainstream classroom, the faster they will learn the language.

☐ Children who have the ability to memorize grammar rules and complete pages of grammar drills will learn to speak and write English more quickly.

☐ Children learn a second language faster and more easily than teenagers and adults do.

☐ The emotional state of the learner doesn't interfere with the acquisition of a new language. As long as English language learners (ELLs) receive instruction from classroom teachers, they will learn English.

☐ Students should be strongly encouraged to speak English from the first day.

Did you guess that all the above statements are false? To provide a successful learning environment for English language learners, classroom teachers and administrators need to understand six essential concepts that are directly related to the statements listed above: culture shock, comprehensible input and output, language acquisition versus language learning, the optimum age for learning a second language, the affective filter, and the silent period. As we explore these concepts, we will also look at classroom scenarios that exemplify each belief.

Culture Shock

True or False? *My newcomer should be referred to the child study team. He is often disruptive in the classroom and kicks and hits the other children. There is something wrong with him aside from not knowing the language.* **FALSE.**

Newcomers who act out in the classroom are most likely suffering from culture shock. Anthropologist Kalvero Oberg first used the term "culture shock" in 1960 to describe the feelings that people have when they move to an unfamiliar culture. What does culture shock look like in immigrant children? They may become withdrawn and passive or they may be more aggressive. The greater the difference between the student's new culture and the student's primary culture, the greater the shock (Levine & Adelman, 1993). Newcomers have usually left behind family members, friends, teachers, and pets. They are no longer surrounded by a familiar language and culture. Children often do not have the full support of their parents because the parents are experiencing culture shock, too. In the following example, Eduardo, an ELL from Mexico, shows his frustration with his new environment.

➡ Eduardo, who is a Mexican newcomer at his elementary school, hits and kicks his classmates. He is frustrated and cries easily. One day, the only other Spanish-speaking student in his

2

class was absent and Eduardo couldn't communicate at all. He threw himself on the floor and screamed. His anger and unhappiness were apparent. His teacher feels that there is something wrong with him beyond the language barrier.

While Eduardo was very affected by his new environment, every child reacts differently to moving to a new place. Most English language learners go through four stages of culture shock before they become comfortable with their new language.

1. Euphoric or Honeymoon Stage. During this stage, newcomers are excited about their new lives. Everything is wonderful and they are having a great time learning about their environment.

2. Rejection Stage. At this stage, the differences between the new culture and the old one become more apparent to newcomers. They reject their new surroundings because there is so much that they do not understand. ELLs can feel overwhelmed and may seem sleepy, irritable, uninterested, or depressed. Students at the rejection stage may refuse to learn the new language. Some students may become aggressive and act out their frustrations like the students in the next example.

> ➡ Ilya, a 10-year-old boy from Russia, clings to his mother's car door and screams when she drops him off at school. Eight-year-old Amir from Lebanon gets sick every day before lunch and has to go home. Rosa, a six-year-old from Puerto Rico, runs wild in her 1st grade classroom because she doesn't understand the classroom rules and expectations.

3. Regression Stage. English language learners are frustrated because they cannot communicate and are bombarded with unfamiliar surroundings, unreadable social signals, and an unrelenting barrage of new sounds. They are homesick and miss their family, friends, and familiar sights and sounds. They spend their leisure time socializing with friends who speak the same language or listening to music and watching videos from their home country.

Teenage newcomers often feel angry and helpless because they have had no say in their families' move to the United States. They have lost control of their environment because they don't speak English. Student essays give us a further glimpse of how newcomers feel when they first come to the United States. One student exclaimed, "I didn't want to leave my country. My parents decided to come here. I didn't have a choice." Another asserted, "I miss my friends and school. I had to leave my grandparents behind." A third student complained, "I eat lunch alone every day. I don't have any friends in this school." Newcomers in this stage of culture shock need time and patience from their teachers.

4. Integration Stage. At this stage, newcomers start to deal with the differences between the old and new cultures. They learn to integrate their own beliefs into their new environment and begin to find ways to exist with both cultures. Many immigrant parents become alarmed at this stage because they do not want their children to lose their primary language and culture, such as the Nakamuras in the next example.

> ➡ The Nakamuras are a Japanese family with four children. They came to the United States for a five-year job-related stay. Because the nearest Japanese school was over an hour away, the children were enrolled in the local public school. Mr. and Mrs. Nakamura did not want their children to become "Americanized." They did not allow them to socialize with classmates after school or join any school groups or clubs. The children were required to come home every day to complete a few hours of homework assigned by the Japanese Saturday School. Needless to say, the children never got past the integration stage, and they were never comfortable with American culture.

5. Acceptance Stage. Newcomers are now able to enter and prosper in the mainstream culture. They accept both cultures and combine them into their lives. Some students will adopt the mainstream culture at school and follow the values of the home culture outside school. During this stage, many immigrant parents make it

4

clear to their children that they do not want them to abandon their primary language and culture. Their concerns are valid, as demonstrated by the family in the following example.

➡ Guadaloupe and Francisca, two sisters from Venezuela, feel pulled between American and Venezuelan cultures and are angry that their parents restrict them from participating in after-school social activities. Guadaloupe was not permitted to attend a school dance and Francisca was not allowed to go to a sleepover party. The girls are also losing their native language. When family members come from their home country, they can understand what is said in Spanish, but they can no longer speak the language.

Comprehensible Input and Output

True or False? *The more time students spend soaking up English in the mainstream classroom, the faster they will learn the language.* **FALSE.**

Students do not simply "soak up" language. Learners must understand the communication that is conveyed by their classmates and teachers. Comprehensible input is a hypothesis proposed by Stephen Krashen (1981) that is widely recognized by today's researchers and practitioners. He suggests that English language learners acquire language by hearing and understanding messages that are slightly above their current English language level. For example, an English language learner may understand the phrase "Put your book in your desk." By slightly changing the phrase to "Put your book on the table," the speaker scaffolds new information that increases the learner's language comprehension. To do this, the teacher must provide new material that builds on the learner's prior knowledge. When newcomers spend most of their day in a mainstream classroom, it is especially critical for them to receive comprehensible input from their teachers and classmates.

If teachers use a lecture style for instruction, the English language learner will not receive as much comprehensible input.

Research shows that English language learners need opportunities to practice language at their level of competency (Pica et al., 1989, 1996; Swain & Lapkin, 1995). When ELLs are able to refine their English skills with their English-speaking peers, this process is called comprehensible output. Many researchers assert that comprehensible output is nearly as important as comprehensible input. Cooperative learning groups are one way for newcomers to receive ample input and output. A small-group setting allows ELLs to have more comprehensible input because classmates modify or adapt the message to the listener's needs. There are more opportunities for oral practice and for repetition of information as peers help newcomers negotiate meaning. Student conversation in a small group is centered on what is actually happening at the moment as the task is completed. Feedback and correction for ELLs are nonjudgmental and immediate. In the next scenario, one history teacher's cooperative learning groups helped his ELLs soar.

➡ English language learners in the 7th grade were placed in Mr. Garcia's American History class. He divided the class into cooperative learning groups and the ELLs blossomed. They were assigned tasks in their small groups that were at their level of English language ability. Many of these students felt that this was the first time they were really a part of the academic life of a content class. Mr. Garcia observed that his ELLs worked much harder in their content-area subjects so that they could be an active part of their group.

Language Acquisition and Language Learning

True or False? *Children who have the ability to memorize grammar rules and complete pages of grammar drills will learn to speak and write English more quickly.* **FALSE.**

Krashen (1988) makes an important distinction between language acquisition and language learning. Children acquire a second language through a subconscious process during which they are unaware of grammatical rules. This process is similar to how they acquire their first language. They get a feel for what is and what isn't correct. To acquire language, the learner needs a source of natural communication. Young students who are in the process of acquiring English can get on-the-job practice by communicating with their classmates.

Language learning, on the other hand, is not communicative. This type of learning comes from direct instruction about the rules of language. Learners have conscious knowledge of the new language and can talk about what they know. They can memorize the rules of the language and perhaps succeed on a standardized test, but they still may not have strong speaking or writing skills. The next example shows how ELLs can perform in the classroom but fail to translate that success into English comprehension.

➡ Yiming is a 4th grader who attended "cram" school in the evening. She learned to read and write by rote memorization. She could sound out words phonetically, fill in grammar pages, regurgitate information in English, and speak without an accent. With this kind of performance in the classroom, Yiming's parents were surprised when her teacher told them that her reading comprehension was low and her creative writing was unintelligible.

The Optimum Age for Language Learning

True or False? *Children learn a second language faster and more easily than teenagers and adults do.* **FALSE.**

This statement is more complex than it seems. In reviews of controlled research (Collier, 1988; Samway & McKeon, 1999) where young children were compared with teenagers and young adults, the teenagers and young adults learned a second language more readily. Children under the age of 8 may outperform adults in the areas of social language and pronunciation because they usually have more occasions to interact socially. The requirements for communication are lower for younger students because they have less language to learn when they interact in a school setting with their peers. Teenagers and adults, on the other hand, have acquired language learning and study skills. They use both acquisition and learning strategies to become fluent in their new language. Compare the English language learning of Priyanka and her younger brother, Nahir.

➡ Seventeen-year-old Priyanka and 7-year-old Nahir arrived from India one year ago. Nahir speaks very fluent social English. His accent is near native. He has made an excellent social adjustment to his 1st grade class and has many friends from different backgrounds. Because he had just begun learning how to read in his native country, he has limited language literacy skills in his first language. Despite his fluent social English, he is experiencing difficulty reading and writing in English and is not doing well in his content-area work. Priyanka, on the other hand, is shy and does not speak much. She has only a few friends and they all speak Gujarati, one of the major languages spoken in India and Pakistan. Her spoken English is heavily accented. Priyanka was an excellent student in India, and she continues to study diligently. She is very successful in her academic studies in the United States and is receiving good grades.

The Affective Filter

True or False? *The emotional state of the learner doesn't interfere with the acquisition of a new language. As long as ELLs receive comprehensible output, they will learn English.* **FALSE.**

Although comprehensible input is necessary for language acquisition, it is not sufficient by itself. The learner's emotional state or affective filter can interfere with acquiring a new language because it involves public practice and speaking in front of others.

These skills require that the learner take a risk. This risk can produce embarrassment and anxiety that can block the learner's ability to process new information (Krashen, 1981; Krashen & Terrell, 1983). To counteract students' affective filter, classroom teachers can create an effective learning environment for ELLs that helps them integrate into the life of the school. They can provide a classroom experience that is nonthreatening and demonstrate to their students that they understand their needs. The key is to make ELLs feel welcome and comfortable so that their affective filter does not impede their learning. In the next example, Ms. Lautz helps one of her ELL students become acclimated to the school environment.

➡ Ms. Lautz immediately pairs her new English language learner with a buddy and encourages her students to become friends with him. She arranges for classmates to stay with the newcomer at lunch, hang around with him on the playground, and help him on the school bus. She also encourages her ELL to participate in extracurricular activities such as sports and music programs.

The Silent Period

True or False? *Students should be strongly encouraged to speak English from the first day.* ***FALSE.***

Most new English language learners will go through a silent period during which they are unable or unwilling to communicate orally in the new language. This stage may last for a few days to more than a year, depending on a variety of factors. The silent period occurs before ELLs are ready to produce oral language and is generally referred to as the preproduction stage of language learning. ELLs should not be forced to speak before they are ready. Teachers shouldn't embarrass these students by putting them on the spot. ELLs need time to listen to others speak, to digest what they hear, to develop receptive vocabulary, and to observe their classmates' interactions. This silent behavior does not mean that students are not learning; however, it may be that they are not ready to speak.

Teacher instruction is an important factor in how long the silent period lasts. If the teacher provides hands-on activities and encourages students to interact in small groups, ELLs will be able to participate in the classroom sooner and be more confident about speaking with their peers. Teachers should not assume that young ELLs would not be embarrassed or shy when attempting to speak a second language.

Another factor that may influence the length of the silent period is the child's personality. If the child is shy or self-conscious, he or she may be reluctant to speak. On the other hand, an outgoing child will speak more readily and will advance more quickly from preproduction to early production. There are also cultural factors to consider. Students, like Arlana in the next example, do not like to make mistakes and will not speak until they have a good grasp of the language.

➡ Arlana, a Muslim student from Lebanon, is in the 2nd grade. She has frustrated every teacher she has worked with since kindergarten. She rarely speaks in English and she has been in school in the United States since the age of 3. When she does respond to her teacher's questions, she whispers. She doesn't talk much to classmates and spends most of her time outside school with family and other Muslim children. Arlana understands oral directions, and she reads and writes on the 2nd grade level. Nothing her teachers have done has made her comfortable about expressing herself orally. Her teachers encouraged her parents to arrange play dates for Arlana with her native English-speaking peers. Her parents were also encouraged to seek professional help for Arlana, but the family moved at the end of 2nd grade and her teachers never saw a resolution to her reticence to speak.

Although this is an extreme example, girls from some cultural backgrounds are not encouraged to speak. Being very quiet in the classroom is often viewed as culturally appropriate behavior for girls.

Native language also plays a role in students' willingness to talk. If the sound systems between their native and second language are similar, students will usually speak earlier.

Differences in language styles among social classes also influence how quickly students speak. Urban middle-class parents tend to speak more, teach verbally, and give oral instructions to even very young children. Newcomers from less industrialized countries teach their children by showing them what to do. They are less likely to verbalize their instructions.

Should mainstream educators know the factors that affect second-language acquisition? If the above beliefs are not dispelled, educators cannot provide an optimum learning environment for English language learners with rich language acquisition opportunities and supportive teachers and classmates.

· · ·

Let's take another look at these beliefs and review what we learned from this chapter: /

* A newcomer who exhibits disruptive or odd behavior may be suffering from culture shock.
* English language learners need comprehensible input. They cannot learn English by "soaking up" language in a mainstream classroom.
* To acquire a new language, children need a source of natural communication. Memorizing grammar rules will not help them learn to speak and write English quickly.
* Children do not learn a second language faster and easier than adults. Their only advantage is in pronunciation.
* The emotional state of English language learners affects how they acquire a new language. ELLs need a comfortable environment in which to learn.

• Newcomers will go through a silent period during which they will not speak. They should not be forced to speak until they are ready.

In this first chapter, we looked at six beliefs about second-language acquisition and explored the key concepts that disprove these beliefs. We examined the concepts of culture shock, comprehensible input and output, language acquisition and learning, age differences, the affective filter, and the silent period. Implications for teachers' instruction were also discussed. Each concept was illustrated with a classroom scenario.

2

How Students Acquire Social and Academic Language

Some of the most pressing and frequent questions administrators, board members, and classroom teachers ask are "How long should it take a newcomer to learn English?" and "What kinds of programs help ELLs acquire English quickly?" In this chapter, we explore the answers to these questions, analyze the essential theories in second-language acquisition, and examine the differences between social and academic English.

As you read the statements below, decide whether you think they are true or false.

☐ English language learners need one to three years to master social language in the classroom.

☐ Students don't always acquire social language naturally in informal contexts. They may need to be taught how to communicate appropriately in social situations.

☐ Although English language learners may speak English on the playground, this does not mean they have mastered the academic and cognitive language of the classroom.

☐ Learning academic subjects in their native language helps ELLs learn English.

☐ Parents of English language learners should be encouraged to speak their primary language at home.

☐ Students who have strong literacy skills in their native language will learn English faster.

☐ Students need more than two to three years in bilingual or ESL classes to succeed in school.

Social Language and the English Language Learner

True or False? *English language learners need one to three years to master social language in the classroom.* **TRUE.**

Social language is the language of the playground. Researcher Jim Cummins calls this language Basic Interpersonal Communication Skills or BICS (Cummins, 1981, 1996). Newcomers use BICS to function socially in hallways, classrooms, school buses, and playgrounds. Cummins's research shows that it takes one to three years for English language learners to reach the social language level of their peers.

The context of social language is embedded. For example, if a student wants a drink of water, he can ask for it by making a drinking motion and saying the word *water*. Newcomers have support for BICS because they can use gestures, objects, and pictures to help make the information comprehensible. English language learners who are in the beginning stages are able to handle the following tasks:

• Produce survival vocabulary such as the words for *water* or *bathroom.*

• Follow simple directions that are accompanied by gestures such as "Point to the door" or "Walk to the chair."

• Engage in one-to-one social conversation using gestures.

• Answer low-level questions such as "Is an elephant large or small?" or "What color is the chair?"

• Participate effectively in hands-on classes such as art and physical education.

- Play uncomplicated games, particularly games that they play well in their native language, such as checkers, chess, or backgammon.
- Produce simple drawings, charts, and graphs.

Context-Reduced Social Language Activities

As we learned in the previous section, social interactions are usually context embedded. These interactions occur in meaningful social settings and most likely they are not cognitively demanding. As your newcomers' listening and oral language skills start to develop, they will be able to add more challenging activities to their repertoire and the context and social cues for these interactions will be reduced. Some context-reduced social language activities include the following:

- Holding predictable conversations with teachers and peers. For example, the student might tell the teacher during a math lesson, "I don't understand." The teacher can demonstrate the math concept using manipulatives and drawings to help the student comprehend.
- Decoding simple reading passages. ELLs will be able to sound out words, but they may not comprehend what they are reading.
- Copying words and sentences from the board.
- Reading a weekly school schedule or a homework assignment.
- Listening to and understanding a simple story.
- Responding to and writing answers for short informational questions. For example, for a history unit on the Pilgrims, a teacher can test literal comprehension by asking, "What was name of the Pilgrims' ship?
- Executing answers to questions about a chart or map, such as "Find Mexico on the map and label it."

- Understanding and communicating knowledge about math facts. At this stage, however, students will not be ready to learn difficult math concepts.
- Interacting socially with classmates. English language learners should be able to ask for help with their schoolwork or understand a teacher's instructions for a game.

Newcomers will be able to participate in context-reduced activities during their content-area classes as well. These activities include science experiments, content-related craft projects, and language arts assignments involving drawings, bookmarks, book covers, and dioramas.

How Do Students Acquire Social Language?

True or False? *Students don't always acquire social language naturally in informal contexts. They may need to be taught how to communicate appropriately in social situations.* **TRUE.**

Does social language need to be taught and practiced or do students pick it up automatically on the playground or in the lunchroom? English language learners may need to be specifically taught interpersonal skills such as how to greet people, give and receive compliments, apologize, and make polite requests. They also need to understand nonverbal language and the use of personal space. The goal of Standard 1 of the 2006 PreK–12 English language proficiency standards is for ELLs to learn to communicate in English for social and instructional purposes during the school day. This goal is important because many ELLs need to learn the appropriate voice tones, volume, and language for different school settings. For example, some ELLs speak to a teacher in the same way that they talk to a peer, such as Min Ki in the next example.

➡ Min Ki is a beginning ELL from Korea. Although his English is quite limited, Min Ki is adept at picking up expressions on the playground. During recess one day he learned to say "Yeah, yeah, yeah." Whenever Ms. Chen, his classroom teacher, gave directions, Min Ki would reply, "Yeah, yeah, yeah." The teacher finally had to ask an adult volunteer to explain to him that this is inappropriate language for a child to use with an adult. In this setting, an adult had to teach Min Ki that there is a difference between language used with an adult and language used with friends on the playground.

Another example of improper language in the classroom is swearing. ELLs may pick up inappropriate language on the playground and may not realize why this language is not suitable in the classroom. In the next example, Vadim's teacher tries to convey the seriousness of his inappropriate language.

➡ Vadim, a 4th grade student from Russia, used an X-rated expression in the classroom. The teacher was understandably distressed and made Vadim write an apology letter for homework. The teacher became even more upset when Vadim's parents did not take the infraction seriously. What the teacher did not know, however, was that Vadim's parents were not appalled because swearing does not have the same shock value in a person's second language as it does in a person's first language.

Many newcomers in middle school and high school say that they are learning academic language but have few opportunities to practice social language. Most of their social interactions are with students with the same native language background. In the next example, we look at Carmen and Diego and their social language skills.

➡ Carmen is an English language learner from the Dominican Republic who attends a suburban middle school. She is a very good student who works hard and has quickly acquired academic English; however, she socializes only with classmates who speak Spanish. Her social language in English is slow and hesitant. She has difficulty initiating a conversation in English. Her Brazilian classmate Diego, on the other hand, is athletic and plays soccer with the boys from his class. Because Diego interacts with many English-speaking teammates, his social English is quite fluent.

Social language comes easier to students who have real reasons to speak with their classmates. Organized school activities such as sports teams, band, or chorus can expose ELLs to social English.

Role playing, teacher modeling, peer modeling, and videos are all good tools for teaching ELLs social skills. Teachers can encourage newcomers to observe their peers as models of correct behavior. Teachers should set expectations for these behaviors by using real incidents that come up in the class such as having students practice saying good morning and good-bye to their teachers and classmates. In the next example, Mrs. Arena teaches her students simple language for social interactions.

➡ Mrs. Arena is a kindergarten teacher who stands at her classroom door at the end of the day. She shakes hands and says good-bye to students as they leave. She uses each child's name and intersperses her farewells with comments. A typical exchange might be:
"Good-bye, Juan. Have fun at the park," Mrs. Arena says.
"Good-bye, Mrs. Arena," replies Juan. "See you tomorrow."

Mrs. Arena makes an everyday classroom routine a valuable lesson in social interaction and small talk. As students leave the playground after school, they say good-bye to each other using the same farewells modeled earlier by the teacher.

Evaluating the Silent Period

How does a teacher know when a child is ready to speak? When should an ELL be encouraged to participate in the standard social language of the classroom?

Mi Yeon is a Korean student who has been in the United States for 18 months. Although she is progressing in her academic work, she barely speaks to her teachers. Even when prompted, she will not say good morning or good-bye to them when she enters and leaves the classroom. One of her teachers, Mrs. Burns-Paterson, has not forced the issue because she knows about the silent period and does not want to traumatize Mi Yeon. Let's take a look at how Mrs. Burns-Paterson helps guide Mi Yeon through the silent period.

> ➡ Mrs. Burns-Paterson decided to set realistic expectations for routine social exchanges in the classroom. She didn't want to single Mi Yeon out, so she gradually added lessons in social language for the whole class. She began by explaining that when they entered the classroom each day, everyone was going to say hello or good morning to the teacher and to the students who sat at their table. She asked several children to act out the greeting. After a week, Mi Yeon successfully participated in this activity.
>
> To further help shy students like Mi Yeon, Ms. Burns-Paterson had her students practice giving compliments. The comments had to be positive and could not be about a classmate's appearance. Students brainstormed a list of compliments they could give each other, such as "I like the way you drew that dinosaur" or "Your handwriting is so neat" or "Your story was interesting. I liked the part where you chased the dog."

We have seen how social language is informally acquired through interactions in classrooms, hallways, cafeterias, and on school buses. Although some social language needs to be modeled and reinforced by the teacher and native English speakers, other social interactions can be picked up by frequent interactions.

Understanding How Students Acquire Academic Language

True or False? *Although English language learners may speak English on the playground, this does not mean they have mastered the academic and cognitive language of the classroom.* **TRUE.**

Teachers and administrators may decide to move students who have social communication skills out of language support services because they sound like native English speakers. ELLs who speak English well in social situations, however, are not necessarily prepared for academic tasks in the classroom. It is crucial for educators to understand the difference between BICS and Cognitive Academic Language Proficiency (CALP).

CALP includes language for formal academic learning and for written texts in content areas such as English literature, math, science, and social studies. CALP skills also encompass reading, writing, and thinking about subject-area content material. Students also use CALP skills to compare, classify, synthesize, evaluate, and infer.

Consider this conversation between Mrs. Perez, an 8th grade history teacher, and Carlota, a student from Mexico.

➡ **Mrs. Perez:** Why didn't you do your homework, Carlota? You're going to fail this class.

➡ **Carlota:** I go visit my aunt. She sick. She got something bad with her heart. My uncle drive my mother and me. We bring aunt some food. When I get home, it's too late finish homework.

Carlota's social language is good. She is able to clearly tell Mrs. Perez what happened. Although Carlota makes some errors, they do not impede communication. In contrast, however, Carlota is not doing well in history and her other academic subjects. She has acquired social language, but she still needs help with her academic vocabulary.

Cognitive academic language skills are both abstract and context reduced. Information can be read from a textbook or presented by the teacher with few verbal cues to help students grasp its meaning. Some ELLs struggle to comprehend what they read and have difficulty expressing what they know in writing.

Many students can say all the words in a reading passage and memorize the definitions of vocabulary words but still not comprehend the text. CALP is more than understanding vocabulary and learning academic facts for a test; it also requires students to sharpen their cognitive abilities and learn new concepts.

As students progress in school, teachers are more likely to present material in a lecture format. The content also becomes more cognitively demanding and the vocabulary becomes more specific to each subject area. New ideas and concepts are presented to the students at the same time as the context-reduced language. Textbooks may be written beyond the language level of an English language learner. ELLs may also have limited background knowledge for subjects such as U.S. history. An instructor's teaching style can also affect how English language learners develop CALP skills. Let's compare Carlota's science teacher, Mr. Angelo, with her history teacher, Mrs. Perez.

➡ Mrs. Perez gives reading assignments in a textbook that is written above Carlota's English language ability. She presents material by lecturing in front of the classroom. Her tests are not modified for the English language learners in the classroom and she provides very little support for ELLs. On the other hand, Mr. Angelo, Carlota's science teacher, uses simple language to introduce new concepts to his students. He outlines the most important information on the chalkboard. ELLs are given the important vocabulary for the lesson with simple definitions. Students are engaged in group work with partners. To help students prepare for tests, Mr. Angelo gives students a study guide. Needless to say, Carlota's progress in science far exceeds her progress in history.

Connecting Languages

True or False? *Learning academic subjects in their native language helps ELLs learn English.* **TRUE.**

Another concept that is generally accepted in the field of second-language acquisition is Cummins's Common Underlying Proficiency (CUP) theory. This model shows the relationship between native language and second language. Cummins says, "Concepts are most readily developed in the first language and, once developed, are accessible through the second language. In other words, what we learn in one language transfers into the new language" (Freeman & Freeman, 1994, p. 176).

This model, often referred to as the "Iceberg Model," is shown in Figure 2.1 (Cummins, 2000). The model shows two peaks above the waterline. One peak represents a student's social language in the primary language and the other peak represents a student's social language in English. Beneath the waterline is one solid iceberg. One side shows a student's academic language proficiency in the primary language and the other side shows academic language proficiency in English. In the middle you can see

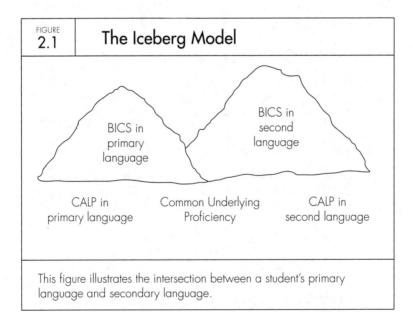

| FIGURE 2.1 | The Iceberg Model |

BICS in primary language

BICS in second language

CALP in primary language

Common Underlying Proficiency

CALP in second language

This figure illustrates the intersection between a student's primary language and secondary language.

Source: Adapted from *Language, power, and pedagogy: Bilingual children in the crossfire* by J. Cummins, 2000. Buffalo, NY: Multilingual Matters, Ltd.

where academic proficiency in English and the primary language intersect. The overlapping area is called Common Underlying Proficiency (CUP).

Using a Primary Language at Home

True or False? *Parents of English language learners should be encouraged to speak their primary language at home.* **TRUE.**

School administrators and classroom teachers should encourage parents to speak their native language at home. It is much more beneficial for children to hear fluent native language with a rich vocabulary than it is to hear imperfect, halting English. We learned from the Iceberg Model that academic concepts learned in students' primary language will help them acquire English. In the next example, Isobel and her family try to integrate English into their home life.

> ➡ Isobel's family is from Costa Rica. Her parents speak some English and are literate in Spanish. When Isobel's teacher told them that they should speak English at home, her parents became distressed. They tried to speak English with her at the dinner table, but their conversations were stilted. Isobel's parents no longer felt comfortable asking her about her school, classes, and homework in Spanish. They stopped discussing books and the television news with her. Although the family reverted to their native language at the dinner table after a week of hesitant English, Isobel felt ashamed of her native language. She wished her parents spoke English.

What Isobel's teacher and parents did not know was that by reading and discussing stories with her and by encouraging Isobel to share her school experiences in Spanish, they were giving her experiences in their native language. Informal conversations like these are critical for Isobel because they will help her establish values and discuss ideas that she is not ready to learn in English. Eventually, what she learns in Spanish will help promote her English proficiency. The concepts and skills that students learn in one language will transfer to the second language when the learner is ready.

Students who are literate in their native language have many skills to draw on when they learn academic English, even when the writing system is different. It is more difficult to teach a concept if it does not exist in the student's native language. Once students grasp the underlying literacy skills of one language, they can use these same skills to learn another language. For example, 10th graders who are literate in Spanish will understand the underlying process of reading in English. Older students will be able to transfer skills such as scanning, selecting important information, predicting what comes next, and visualizing to enhance comprehension. Younger children who are literate in one language will know that printed words carry meaning, that words can be combined into sentences and paragraphs, and that certain letters stand for certain sounds. Regardless of students' age, a new concept will be difficult to teach if it doesn't exist in the students' native language. Let's take a look at Xiang and her progress in her English class.

> ➡ Xiang is a 6th grade student from China who has been in the United States for three years. Her teacher, Mrs. Rahmin, worries that Xiang does not use articles, plurals, or pronouns. Her verb tenses are usually incorrect. She consistently leaves the *s* off plural words. Xiang's parents report that she is literate in Mandarin, a Chinese language.

Mrs. Rahmin does not understand that Chinese languages do not have morphological changes to show case, number, and tense. For example, there is no subject-verb agreement and there are no markings at the end of words to denote plurals. There are also no Chinese words that translate into *a, an,* or *the.* Because of these differences, it is very difficult for Xiang to master the grammatical features of English that do not exist in Chinese.

How Long Does It Take Students to Learn English?

True or False? *Students who have strong literacy skills in their native language will learn English faster.* ***TRUE.***

Classroom teachers, administrators, and school board members frequently ask, "How long does it take a student to learn English?" and "How long should students receive language support?" Let's look at the research.

The most comprehensive research available on English language learners was conducted by Thomas and Collier (1997). They studied the language acquisition of 700,000 English language learners in a longitudinal study from 1982 to 1996. They wanted to find out how long it would take for students with no background in English to reach the performance of a native speaker on norm-referenced tests (50th percentile). In addition, they looked at variables such as socioeconomic status, students' first language, programs used to learn English, and the amount of formal schooling in students' primary language.

Thomas and Collier found that the most significant variable in how long it takes for a student to learn English is *the amount of formal schooling students receive in their first language.*

In one part of the study, Thomas and Collier researched a group of Asian and Hispanic students from an affluent suburban school district. These students received one to three hours of second-language support per day in a well-regarded ESL program. These students generally exited the ESL program in the first two years. All students were at or above grade level in native language literacy. For this group, Thomas and Collier found these results:

• Students ages 8 to 11 years old with two to three years of native language education took five to seven years to test at grade level in English.

- Students with little or no formal schooling who arrived in the United States before the age of 8 took 7 to 10 years to reach grade-level norms in English language literacy.
- Students who were below grade level in their native language also took 7 to 10 years to reach the 50th percentile. Many of these students never reached grade-level norms.

These data held true regardless of the home language, country of origin, or socioeconomic status.

Which Program Works?

True or False? *Students need more than two or three years in bilingual or ESL classes to succeed in school.* ***TRUE.***

Many ESL educators believe that English language learners who receive a specific ESL service acquire English faster than students in other types of programs. However, research does not support this belief. Thomas and Collier found that English language learners who received all of their schooling in English performed extremely well in kindergarten through 3rd grade, regardless of the type of bilingual or ESL program. These students made dramatic gains in English. However, when they reached the 4th grade and moved through middle school and high school, the performance of students who had been in all-English programs, such as ESL pullouts, fell substantially.

Why did this happen? Native English speakers make an average language gain of 10 months each school year. However, English language learners who had not become literate in their native language, regardless of what that native language was, only made a six- to eight-month gain per school year. As a result, the gap between native English speakers and English language learners in all-English programs widened from the 4th grade through high school (Thomas & Collier, 1997).

Students in two-way bilingual immersion and developmental bilingual programs, however, reach the 50th percentile in both their native language and English by 4th or 5th grade in all subject areas. These students are able to sustain these gains in English, and in some cases they achieve even higher success than native English speakers as they move through their secondary school years.

Bilingual programs are not always more effective than ESL or sheltered content programs. Schools should look beyond a program's label and consider the following:

• Are the assigned teachers qualified to teach English language learners?
• Are there sufficient materials for the program?
• What instructional methods are used?
• Are students exited into all-English programs too quickly?

Cummins says, "Quick-exit transitional bilingual education is an inferior model based on an inadequate theoretical assumption; this model aspires to monolingualism and does little to address the causes of bilingual students' underachievement" (Freeman & Freeman, 1998).

What does this research mean for school administrators and supervisors? Bilingual programs are not always feasible, especially in school districts where students come from multiple language backgrounds. Your district can build a better program by taking these key steps:

• Give students more time to develop English language academic skills. Don't rush younger students through language support programs.
• Provide more support services to underschooled upper elementary and middle school students. Remember that it will take them 7 to 10 years to reach grade-level norms.
• Encourage parents to maintain their native language at home. Promote after-school and Saturday instruction in a first language. If your school district has enough students, push for a developmental bilingual or two-way immersion program.

• Provide a sheltered English program. A sheltered English program uses simplified English to present subject-specific material to English language learners. For more information on these programs, see Chapter 7.

• • •

Let's review the major points from this chapter:

• English language learners need one to three years to master social language skills (BICS) for everyday interactions.

• Students may need to be taught how to communicate appropriately in social situations.

• Newcomers who speak English on the playground are not necessarily fluent in the academic and cognitive language of the classroom.

• Learning academic subjects in their native language helps ELLs learn English.

• Parents of English language learners should be encouraged to speak their native language at home.

• Students who have strong literacy skills in their native language will learn English faster.

• ELLs receiving pullout ESL services do not necessarily make more progress in English than students in dual-language or developmental bilingual programs.

• Students need more than two to three years in bilingual or ESL classes to succeed in school.

In this chapter, we looked at the differences between acquiring social and academic language. We examined how students acquire first and second languages and we showed how the common underlying proficiency (CUP) helps students acquire a second language. Finally, we discussed how long it takes for students to acquire academic language in various types of programs.

3

Correlating Instruction with the Stages of Second-Language Acquisition

In this chapter, we discuss the five stages of language acquisition and how they affect instruction. The characteristics of each stage and suggested activities for students are listed below. We also examine four different learning styles and discuss how they apply to English language learners. Finally, we look at Bloom's taxonomy and consider the six levels of critical thinking skills and what activities English language learners can do at each level.

Stages of Language Acquisition

There are five stages of English language acquisition. It is important to determine the stages of your ELLs so that you can align your instruction with their learning levels. How do you do this? Read the descriptions below to match the language level of your ELLs with the appropriate activities.

Stage 1: Preproduction

This is the silent period discussed in Chapter 1. During this stage, ELLs are acquiring language but they are not yet speaking. They have up to 500 words of receptive vocabulary. Although some students at this stage will repeat everything you say, they are not really producing language. They are simply parroting what they hear.

At this stage, ELLs will listen attentively. They can respond to pictures and other visuals and understand and duplicate gestures and movements to show comprehension. Choral reading and Total Physical Response (TPR) methods will work well for ELLs at this stage. Newcomers will benefit from having a buddy who speaks their native language and translates new words or phrases. Teachers should focus on helping ELLs develop their listening comprehension skills and build a receptive vocabulary. Listening and acquiring a new language can be exhausting for young learners, so teachers should not overwhelm them. Let's take at look at how Mrs. Wondra helps Melik settle into her 1st grade class.

> ➡ Melik is a 1st grader from Turkey. He entered Mrs. Wondra's class a few days before her students presented *The Three Little Pigs* to the other 1st grade classes and their parents. It was too late for Melik to learn the play, but Mrs. Wondra had a bilingual parent explain the story to him and they discovered that he already knew the story in his native language. Melik made a costume and mask out of paper bags with the rest of the class. Mrs. Wondra included Melik in rehearsals and he learned where to stand on the stage and how to make the physical movements and gestures with the group. He also had a buddy stand nearby to help him. Melik felt welcome because Mrs. Wondra included him in this activity.

As Malik repeatedly heard the tale of *The Three Little Pigs*, the language of the story was illustrated through gestures, body movements, and pictures. He not only felt part of the classroom community, but he received comprehensible input for this language. As a result, Malik quickly moved on to the next stage of language acquisition.

Stage 2: Early Production

This stage can last up to six months and students will develop both a receptive and an active vocabulary of about 1,000 words.

A student's active vocabulary includes the words that students use in speaking or writing as opposed to their receptive vocabulary which contains the words that they understand when used by others.

During this stage, students can usually speak in one- or two-word phrases. They can memorize and use short language chunks, although they may not use them correctly, as you can see with the students in Miss Horne's class in the next example.

➡ English language learners in Miss Horne's 1st grade class learned how to use specific holiday greetings. As they left school one Friday afternoon in December, they called out to their teacher, "Bye, Happy Thanksgiving." These students had correctly memorized the expression, but they did not realize that the greeting was used only for a specific holiday.

Below are suggestions for working with students during this stage of English language acquisition.

- Ask yes/no and either/or questions.
- Accept one- or two-word responses.
- Give students opportunities to participate in whole-class activities.
- Use picture books and realia (i.e., real items) to support language development.
- Modify content information for the language level of ELLs.
- Build vocabulary with visual support.
- Provide listening activities.
- Expose students to print and use simple books with predictable text.
- Support students' learning with graphic organizers, charts, and graphs.
- Begin fostering students' writing in English through labeling and short sentences; use a framework to scaffold writing.
- Use Total Physical Response (TPR) and Language Experience Approach (LEA) (see Chapter 7).

Stage 3: Speech Emergence

At this stage, students have developed an active and receptive vocabulary of 3,000 words and can communicate with simple phrases and short sentences. They can ask simple questions, which may or may not be grammatically correct, such as "May I go to bathroom?" ELLs can also initiate short conversations with their classmates. They will be able to understand easy stories that they read in class with the support of pictures. They will also be able to do some content work with support. Teachers should begin teaching learning strategies and study skills. Here are some simple tasks they can complete during this phase:

- Sound out stories phonetically.
- Read short, modified texts in content-area subjects.
- Understand simplified content materials.
- Learn key vocabulary and concepts.
- Complete graphic organizers with word banks.
- Understand and answer questions about charts and graphs.
- Match vocabulary words with their definitions.
- Study flash cards with content-area vocabulary.
- Participate in duet, paired, and choral reading activities.
- Write and illustrate riddles.
- Understand teacher explanations and two-step directions.
- Compose brief stories based on personal experience.
- Listen to books on tape.
- Write in dialogue journals.

It's important for ELLs to have a place to express their thoughts and ideas. Dialogue journals are good tools to help spark conversation between the teacher and the student. These journals are especially helpful with English language learners. Students can write about topics that interest them and proceed at their own rate. Let's consider how Mrs. Kargauer uses dialogue journals with her students.

> ➡ Mrs. Kargauer knew that her 10th grade students from Ecuador had many questions about their new culture, but they were too shy to ask. She introduced dialogue journals to all of her students, which provided a safe outlet for them to ask their questions. Because their writing was not critiqued or graded, the students felt comfortable writing to the teacher. They loved having the individual attention and Mrs. Kargauer learned important information about them.

Mrs. Kargauer extends this personal connection with her students during the summer. Every June, she takes a photo of each student, which she then sends to them with a short note in July. In the note she encourages her students to write back to her.

Stage 4: Intermediate Fluency

English language learners at the intermediate fluency stage have a vocabulary of 6,000 active words. They are beginning to use more complex sentences when speaking and writing and are willing to express opinions and share their thoughts. They will ask questions to clarify what they are learning in class. ELLs at this stage will be able to complete work in grade-level math and science classes with some teacher support (as outlined below). Students' comprehension of English literature and social studies content is increasing. At this stage, students will use strategies from their native language to learn content in English. Here are some activities students might complete at this stage.

• Read and understand modified texts in content-area subjects.
• Learn vocabulary and concepts in science and social studies classes with teacher support.
• Answer questions from science and social studies texts.
• Organize information using graphic organizers.

- Highlight important information in a text.
- Provide definitions for vocabulary words.
- Participate in short skits or plays.
- Understand teacher explanations with visual support.
- Write personal stories and journals.

As students try to master the complexity of English grammar and sentence structure, their writing will have many errors. At this stage, they should be able to synthesize what they have learned and make inferences. Students will also be able to understand more complex concepts if teachers help them develop learning strategies. Let's see how Mrs. Millard directs her class in the next example.

➡ Mrs. Millard is a 6th grade teacher who actively involves all her students in developing thinking skills. During a lesson on the founding of early settlements in the Americas, Mrs. Millard wants students to learn to make a time line. She draws a line on the board labeled with the years 1585 through 1825. Six students are chosen to hold posters that describe different events taking place during this time period.

Because there are many English language learners in Mrs. Millard's class this year, the posters also contain a picture of each event. Students are asked to move around to show the correct order of events. When they are satisfied with their order, one student is chosen to read the placards and classmates are asked if they agree with the order of the time line. Students then have an opportunity to ask their classmates to move to a different position.

This activity is visual, kinesthetic, and well suited for English language learners who are at the speech emergence to intermediate fluency stage of language acquisition. By using pictures with the text, the teacher makes the lesson more meaningful for ELLs.

Stage 5: Advanced Fluency

As discussed in Chapter 2, students can take 5 to 10 years to achieve cognitive academic language proficiency in a second language. Students who have reached advanced fluency are close to performing like their native English-speaking peers in their content-area classes. Teachers can help ELLs at the advanced fluency stage in several ways:

- Offer continued support for oral communication by using more complex vocabulary and sentence structure.
- Support independent reading of content-area materials.
- Allow ELLs to use their native language to learn new concepts or vocabulary.
- Help students expand their writing skills; this may be one area where students are still struggling.
- Offer continued support for developing learning strategies and study skills.

Teaching to the Learning Styles of ELLs

It is important for teachers to teach to the learning styles of all their students, but this concept becomes even more crucial when instructing English language learners. ELLs may experience difficulties as they acquire English because they are accustomed to learning through a different style. When newcomers are at the preproduction and early production levels of learning English, they are usually tactile and kinesthetic learners. ELLs who are auditory or visual learners in their native language most likely will not revert to these styles until they are at the intermediate fluency stage. Middle and high school teachers who are used to teaching in a lecture format should be aware that this type of teaching style can be difficult for some ELLs. Teachers need to know how to adjust their classes to different learning styles, as described below.

Auditory Learners

Students who favor auditory learning can recall what they hear, prefer oral instructions, and learn by listening and speaking. These students also enjoy talking, interviewing, reading aloud, choral reading, and listening to recorded books. Auditory learners perform best in these activities:

- Learning in cooperative groups.
- Receiving oral evaluations of their work.
- Having questions read to them on a test.
- Listening to the teacher's explanations of content-area material.
- Participating in oral discussions of written material.

Visual Learners

ELLs who are visual learners benefit from having information presented through visual mediums. They learn best by observing and prefer written instructions. These students are sight readers who enjoy reading silently. Visual learners prefer that information be presented in the following ways:

- Computer graphics
- Maps, graphs, charts, diagrams
- Posters
- Graphic organizers
- Text with pictures
- Key points of lesson on chalkboard

Tactile Learners

Students with tactile strength learn best by touching. They understand directions that they can write and they enjoy using manipulatives to learn new concepts. Try using the Language Experience Approach (LEA) when teaching tactile learners to read. Tactile learners work well with these activities:

- Drawing and labeling.
- Writing down content material.
- Playing board games.
- Making models and dioramas.

- Following diagrams and pictures to construct something.
- Using manipulatives in mathematics (e.g., using coins during a lesson on money).

Let's take a look at how Mrs. Appert uses manipulatives to help the tactile learners in her class.

➡ Mrs. Appert is a basic skills teacher with a good understanding of the needs of English language learners. During her basic skills instruction she provides a variety of tactile experiences for her ELLs. In her class an observer sees students feeling sandpaper numbers, learning how to measure with rice or beans, sorting different kinds of buttons, writing in salt on a tray, or using raised physical maps.

Kinesthetic Learners

Kinesthetic learners are similar to tactile learners because they also learn by touching or manipulating objects, but kinesthetic learners involve their whole body as they learn. Total Physical Response (TPR) is a good learning method for these students. When they act out material, they tend to remember the lesson better. Kinesthetic learners learn best through these activities:

- Playing games that involve their whole body.
- Participating in movement activities and songs with actions.
- Reading chorally with gestures.
- Making models.
- Setting up experiments.
- Acting out short plays and skits.
- Participating in role playing.

In the next example, Mrs. Du Bois uses a kinesthetic activity to help her students learn about the Civil War.

➡ Mrs. Du Bois is a 5th grade teacher who is experienced with English language learners and knows their learning styles. When she started her unit on the Civil War, she divided her room physically into the North and the South. Students sitting on the north side of the room were Northerners who had to find ways to get to the pencil sharpener that was on the south side of the room. Students on the south side were Southerners who needed to negotiate to get the paper or scissors that they needed during the day. Before school started at 8:30, students could come and go freely around the room, but they had to plan their activities for the rest of the day. Some students had friends on the other side of the room who were secretly willing to help them. Others made quick forays to the other side for supplies before they could be captured. Students not only had a kinesthetic way to learn about the Civil War, but they used problem-solving skills to find unique solutions.

Thinking Skills and English Language Learners

To help English language learners develop critical thinking skills, educators can use Bloom's taxonomy, which is a way to classify instructional activities or questions. Teachers need to realize, however, that some of the tasks on the taxonomy are difficult for ELLs because they lack the language and vocabulary to express their thoughts and ideas in English. Teachers should ask themselves, "How far up the scale should a student with this amount of English be able to go?" Then they should ask questions that are age- and language-appropriate for ELLs. Bloom's taxonomy can be used with even very young children. In the examples below, we take a look at what students at the speech-emergent and intermediate fluency levels should be able to do. The examples are from a 5th grade American History unit on the Civil War that will help us visualize how to use Bloom's taxonomy with English language learners.

Level 1: Knowledge

Knowledge-level questions require students to demonstrate their ability to recall previously learned material. Pictures, drawings, and realia will support students in answering these questions. Responses to knowledge-level questions are generally found in the text and students may respond using one-word or short phrases. For example, when teaching students about the Civil War, here are some questions you might ask: "What are the names of two Confederate generals?" or "Where was the first battle fought?" or "Which states were border states?" Students could also list the names of Northern states in the Civil War or label the Confederate states on the map.

Level 2: Comprehension

ESL teachers rely heavily on comprehension questions to assess what students have understood and how students interpret the information they have learned. At this stage, teachers ask students to compare, contrast, illustrate, and classify information by using oral questions and graphic organizers such as Venn diagrams or other comparison charts. As we continue to use our example of the Civil War, here are some activities that ELLs could complete:

• Compare Northern and Southern views on slavery.
• Make a chart of the battles won by the Union and the Confederate armies during the Civil War.
• Make a drawing that shows one key difference in beliefs between people in free states and people in slave states.

Level 3: Application

At the application level, students are learning to solve problems by using previously learned facts in a different way. ELLs might need scaffolding and word banks to learn skills such as building, choosing, constructing, developing, organizing, planning, selecting, solving, and identifying. For example, ask students to write a list of important decisions Americans had to make in 1860 and 1861 or ask them to develop a time line to show the important events leading to the Civil War. They could write a list of questions that they would ask Abraham Lincoln if they could interview him. Students could also make a diorama of a Civil War event and explain their event to the class.

Level 4: Analysis

At the analysis level, students compare and contrast content information and relate it to their personal experiences. This level is difficult for ELLs who may not have enough vocabulary or language to express their responses in English. With some scaffolding from the teacher, however, ELLs will be able to classify, contrast, compare, categorize, and sequence tasks. Ask students to look at a map of Civil War battles and explain why so many battles took place in eastern Virginia. They could also complete a chart comparing differing views on slavery from Abraham Lincoln and Stephen Douglas. They could also create a sequence of the events that helped bring the Civil War to an end.

Level 5: Synthesis

Students are learning to assemble information in a different way at the synthesis level by combining elements in a new pattern or proposing alternative solutions. ELLs need teacher support and scaffolding to answer questions at this level. Synthesis can be particularly difficult for ELLs, but those students who have experience with synthesis in their native language will usually be able to transfer this skill to English. They may be able to use skills such as choosing, combining, creating, designing, developing, imagining, predicting, solving, and changing. Teachers can assign questions and activities such as these:

- Why did Lincoln have to consider different viewpoints before deciding to fight the South?
- How did the Underground Railroad help slaves escape the South?
- Draw a picture of a Civil War hero and explain why you think that person was a hero.
- Northerners did not want Southerners to own slaves. If you were president, how would you solve this problem?

Level 6: Evaluation

Questions at the Evaluation level of Bloom's taxonomy can be modified so that the language is simplified but the task remains the same. Intermediate-level English language learners can learn to give opinions, evaluate the work of an author, or make judgments about events in history. Students should be able to answer the following questions with some scaffolding by the teacher: "What would you do if a friend asked you to make your house a stop on the Underground Railroad?" or "What do you think would have happened if Lincoln had lost the election?" ELLs could also participate in a mock debate about the spread of slavery to the West. Teachers can also ask students to pretend that they are presidential candidates Abraham Lincoln, Stephen Douglas, or John Breckinridge and ask them to defend their stance on slavery.

• • •

In this chapter, we examined the five stages of language acquisition. As we looked at the description of English language learners at each stage, we discussed the types of activities that would help them learn the best. Through these descriptions, classroom teachers will be able to discern the English language level of ELLs in their classes.

We also reviewed four different learning styles and discussed their relevance to diverse learners. Different types of activities were suggested for each of the four styles to help teachers differentiate their instruction. Finally, we considered Bloom's six levels of critical thinking questions and reviewed what types of activities ELLs could accomplish at each level.

4

The Newcomers' First
Weeks of School

If you are a classroom teacher, you may be saying, "All this theory is fine, but the ELLs in my class are newcomers. What do I do with them?" In this chapter, you learn what teachers and administrators can do to help new English language learners. The students described in this chapter have been in the United States for less than six months and are just learning to speak English. They are at the preproduction or early production stage of second-language acquisition. This chapter shows you how to translate theory into classroom practice.

Creating Welcoming Schools for Newcomers

If we want linguistically and culturally diverse students to gain long-term social and academic success, then we must be ready to provide a challenging and enriching educational program that helps them become part of the mainstream learning environment. This initiative should not be isolated but part of a coordinated, districtwide effort.

English language learners should be engaged in meaningful instruction throughout the school day. They need to be involved in their content-areas classes from the first months of school, even though their participation may be limited at first.

What does your district need to do to accommodate the growing number of ELLs in your school system? Many of the suggestions in this chapter can be implemented very inexpensively. Some efforts will require policy changes and support from administrators. Others, such as professional development or native language translations, will require both money and effort.

Establish an Inclusive District Philosophy

Your school district should demonstrate that it values and appreciates the various cultures within your immigrant population. Schools with successful ESL programs have written philosophies that directly state their commitment to recognizing and appreciating the diversity of their students. This philosophy should include your intent to create a comprehensive and supportive environment for all students. For example, differentiating instruction and assessment is one way to make your classroom inclusive. Perhaps your newcomers can't follow a social studies lesson on Pilgrims, but they can learn five concrete vocabulary words from the unit and label a map of the New World. Below are a few tips to help your ELLs feel welcome in your school community.

➡ You can welcome newcomers by making your school walls and decorations reflective of students' native cultures. Classroom items such as a chalkboard, desk, and chair can be labeled in your students' native languages. Displaying pictures of your newcomers' countries and signs in their native languages conveys the message that your school celebrates diversity. Recognizing the holidays of all your students also shows respect for other cultures.

Reducing Your Newcomers' Anxiety

Newcomers should receive additional support during the first few months. An extra 30 minutes per day of instruction makes a huge difference in a student's progress. ESL instruction should begin as soon as students enter school. Students who are not literate in their native language will need to receive literacy instruction in English as well as in their native language. To increase your newcomers' instructional time, you can use a native-language or an English-speaking buddy, cross-grade tutors, and volunteers. After a long day of instruction in English, give your new students a time-out. Let them listen to music from their home countries and give them an opportunity each day during those first weeks to speak with other students from the same native language.

ESL and classroom teachers, administrators, and school office personnel can alleviate some culture shock for newcomers by creating a nurturing environment for them in school. The first few weeks are especially critical. Put yourself in your students' place. Imagine that you have been sent to another country to go to school. You have lost all that is familiar: family, friends, school, home, and even your language. Keep in mind that your newcomers may not receive much support from their parents, who are also experiencing frustrating feelings of culture shock (Claire & Haynes, 1994).

A good relationship with their teachers and classmates is key in helping newcomers cope with their new challenges. Remember the affective filter from Chapter 1? Anxiety can impede students' learning (Krashen, 1985a). If students do not feel secure in school, their learning will be hindered. Conversely, when newcomers have a positive experience in school, they will acquire language faster. Let's look at how Ms. Connell works with ELLs in her classroom.

> ➡ Ms. Connell is a successful classroom teacher of ELLs. She is a warm, friendly person, and she has a relaxed manner that helps reduce her newcomers' anxiety. She knows that her ELLs need encouragement; therefore, she provides opportunities for her students to succeed. Ms. Connell maintains high expectations, but she does not expect her ELLs to work above their English levels. She reevaluates their levels on an ongoing basis.

Provide Training in Diverse Cultures

All certificated staff, including administrators, classroom teachers, special area teachers, school nurses, and child study team members, need training in second-language acquisition, diverse cultures, and culture shock. It is also crucial for your school to provide training in diverse cultures for support staff members. School secretaries, classroom aides, cafeteria workers, playground aides, bus drivers, and custodians contribute greatly to the school atmosphere and they are an important part of establishing a welcoming environment.

When newcomers enter school, it is important to remember that some students may appear to speak English because they have acquired social language (BICS). They may not be prepared to fully participate in the mainstream classroom because they have not acquired academic language (CALP) and therefore require language support. Participation in support programs should not be decided by school secretaries or other office personnel on the basis of a student's social language. It is the ESL or bilingual teacher's job to decide whether a student should be included in your school's ESL or bilingual program.

ESL teachers may also need to provide input on a student's grade placement. School years begin and end at different times of the year in other countries, which may influence grade placement. Also, ELLs should not be retained because of language and should be placed with students of their own age. See how a well-versed school secretary helps place newcomers in the following example.

➡ On the first day of school in September, two students enter a school office. Ha Eun was in the 3rd grade at the end of the school year in Korea and her parents wanted her to go into the 4th grade. Ernesto, on the other hand, had completed 5th grade in Mexico and his parents wanted him to repeat the 5th grade because he didn't speak any English. Fortunately, Mrs. Jennings, the school secretary, had received training in diverse

45

cultures. She knew that schools in Korea start a new school year in April and that Ha Eun had only finished part of the 3rd grade. She placed Ha Eun correctly in the 3rd grade. She also knew that students should not be retained because of language and enrolled Ernesto in the 6th grade.

How a student is welcomed into your school will make a lasting impression. Look at your school from a newcomer's point of view. Are the staff members who meet the newcomers friendly? Do these staff members understand the students' culture? Are bilingual aides or volunteers available to help new students and their parents with registration and to explain school practices? In case of an emergency, is there a list in the main office that shows all the people in the building who speak the newcomer's language?

Learn About Your Newcomers' Language and Culture

Students with diverse linguistic and cultural backgrounds bring a wealth of experiences from their culture to the classroom. These students have unique experiences to share. You can take advantage of this natural resource and use diversity to teach your mainstream students to value the many distinct cultures of the world. Your school district can establish bilingual clubs and hold international celebrations, festivals, and dinners to show support for your newcomers' cultures.

It is important to tie the school curriculum to the cultures of your ELLs. Although your newcomers may not be literate in their own language, they will usually recognize the written form of their language and feel proud that it is displayed in classrooms and hallways (Brush & Haynes, 1999). Ask bilingual students to bring in native language magazines. Have them cut out pictures that represent their culture and hang them in your classroom. If these pictures are laminated, they can be shared among other teachers. These small steps will help your newcomers develop pride in their heritage and will demonstrate that you respect their culture.

Understand Your Students' Names

Avoid the temptation to Americanize a student's name or create a nickname. Immigrant students have already suffered the trauma of leaving behind their extended family members, friends, teachers, and schools. Don't further traumatize your students by calling them by an American name. If the child comes to school with an Americanized name, there is not much you can do, but the school should never Americanize a student's name. It is important to learn how names are used in your students' culture. Here are a few examples:

Korean names are written with the family name, Kang, first and then the given name, Chung Hee, which usually has two parts. Two-part names should not be shortened. Also, Kang Chung Hee's mother does not take her husband's name, but she retains her own family name.

In general, children from Spanish-speaking families have a given name followed by two surnames. The first surname is the father's family name and the second surname is the mother's family name. Schools should not drop either of these surnames. If a child registers as Maria Hernandez Lopez, both the Hernandez and Lopez should be retained. Spanish-speaking families who have lived in the United States awhile will often either hyphenate the double surname or use the father's family name.

Because Hindu names are often very long, family members and friends may shorten a child's name. In school, however, teachers use the formal names. Hindu adults and children do not call anyone who is older by his or her name. A 6-year-old girl will call her 7-year-old brother *Bhaiya,* or *Older Brother,* and he will call her by her first name.

Chinese names are made up of three characters. The first character is the family name and the other two characters are the given name. Families generally give their children two names. One name is a nickname to be used by friends and family and the other is an official name used for the birth certificate and the school. Students are usually called by their full name in school, but friends and close relatives may use just the given name.

In Russia, children have three parts to their names: a given name, a patronymic, and the father's surname. A patronymic is a type of middle name based on the father's first name. If a student named Marina Viktorevna Rakhmaninova enrolls in your school, you can tell that her father's name is Viktor. The *a* at the end of all three names shows that she is female. In American schools, Russian students will often use their given and family names, following American custom (Haynes, 2006).

Get Your Newcomers' Parents Involved

There are many ways to include parents in their child's education, even if they don't speak English. Let's take a look at how Mrs. Murphy and Mrs. Hernandez get their newcomers' parents involved.

➡ Mrs. Murphy is a 2nd grade teacher who studies the cultures of her English language learners and creates opportunities to invite her students' parents into the classroom. Her ELLs flourish when the class studies their respective countries. When the class learned about Japan, Yuki, a shy Japanese student, was on cloud nine. The teacher invited Yuki's parents to visit the classroom during this unit to do a cultural demonstration. Yuki's mother arrived at school wearing a kimono. Her parents taught the students about calligraphy, origami, traditional dress, music, and dance. Yuki keeps a picture book about world cultures, *Children Just Like Me: Celebrations!* (Kindersley, 1997), in her desk, and she looks at the pictures of children from her home country repeatedly during the school day.

➡ Mrs. Hernandez, a 4th grade teacher, taught her class about Mexico and focused on Cinco de Mayo. Students learned songs in Spanish and performed them for their classmates. Carlos, a student from Mexico, brought in pictures of dancers in the streets of Mexico City. His mother helped the class celebrate Cinco de Mayo with Spanish songs and Mexican food. She also showed the students how to make paper flowers to decorate the room for the celebration. Carlos blossomed during this event.

Develop Special Programs for Your Newcomers and Their Families

Many schools and districts offer extra programs for their ESL population such as Saturday school, family literacy classes, adult ESL classes, and bilingual handbooks for parents. A bilingual handbook might contain important information for parents about the school in English and in their native language. Your school or district should also keep a file of standard school communications and school social activities written in your newcomers' native language to send to parents. If there are no native language teachers or aides in your school district, find parents and community members who can help translate and communicate important school information. Another way to help families become acclimated to the school and the community is to hold meetings in the evening to explain school programs to parents. You can encourage more families to attend by offering babysitting services for parents who must bring their children to the meeting. Your school and district can demonstrate respect for your newcomers' families by inviting them to participate in their children's education.

Organizing Your Classroom

Select a corner of your room where you can keep equipment and materials for your new English language learners. Label everything and organize this language learning area so that students, buddies, and volunteers can easily find what they need. Students can work in this area, or they can carry materials back to their desk. You should prominently display a work schedule that includes pictures and page numbers to guide newcomers and their buddies in the work that you want them to do. Students will feel more comfortable when they know what is expected of them and when their school day has a purpose. ELLs should feel free to go to the language learning area to work on these activities when they cannot follow the work being done in the classroom. Please note that many newcomers are too shy to initiate working in the learning center and will require your direction to do so (Claire & Haynes, 1994).

Gather Materials and Supplies

One of the first items you will need is a booklet of activities for brand-new English language learners to complete. Many publishers have books with activity pages for newcomers to help them learn vocabulary for the classroom, weather, seasons, food, clothing, home, and animals (Haynes, 1997). For your newcomers in grades K–6, you'll need a tape player or CD player with earphones for use with recorded books. Try to find simple stories that are read at a slower speed. If you find audiobooks that have been translated into your newcomers' language, have students listen to a story in their native language and then in English. Students should listen to the same story several times. Ask your district to buy language-related interactive computer programs. Programs do not have to be designed specifically for English language learners. There are also many resources on the Internet that will help newcomers practice their English. A search on the Internet will direct you to these many useful sites.

To make your lessons kinesthetic, use realia or manipulatives. You can also include well-illustrated magazines in English and students' native language for cutting out pictures. Students can make collages based on letters of the alphabet, clothing, household items, food, and animals. You can purchase commercial flash cards with pictures to practice vocabulary or you can create your own flash cards by using blank 3" × 5" index cards. Remember, however, that vocabulary is best learned in context. Flash cards should be used as tools to practice the vocabulary learned in a specific context.

English language learners in middle and high schools will need materials relating to content-area instruction. Try to find sheltered versions of your content-area curricula. (A sheltered book has been written at a lower language level, but the concepts have not been simplified.) You can also use texts that have been written specifically for ESL students. Choose books that are well illustrated and have controlled vocabulary. You may need to find nonfiction picture books at the library that cover the same science, health, and social studies materials that you are currently teaching. Make sure the covers on the books you choose are not too juvenile. Your school may want to consider purchasing age-appropriate English/native language dictionaries, stories, and literature books in various languages that span students' reading levels and computer programs that teach English vocabulary and grammar. Many families will want to buy electronic translators for their students.

To further help your ELLs, make graphic organizers for them with key ideas and vocabulary to learn from a specific chapter. When your students gain proficiency in English, teach them how to organize information for themselves on organizers.

Establish a Routine

During the first few weeks of school, everything will be chaotic for your English language learners. Make a schedule to give your students a sense of structure and have them keep it in their ESL notebooks or tape it to their desks. Your English language learners need to be a part of your class. Don't isolate them from their classmates with separate work all day. Allow them to participate at their level in content-area classes.

In the next example, Mrs. Gorman helps Miguel plan his schedule.

➡ Mrs. Gorman, a 2nd grade teacher, gives her newcomer, Miguel, a schedule for each day. She assigns Miguel a buddy to help him get started on each activity. She uses pictures to show words such as *art, computer,* and *listening center,* and she includes his special classes on his schedule. She also has a picture of a clock for the time that each new activity begins. Miguel knows exactly what is expected of him. Here is a sample schedule for Monday morning.

Miguel's Monday Schedule

9:00–9:30	Computer work with CD on farm animals
9:30–10:15	Art class
10:15–10:30	Snack
10:30–11:00	Listen to "Little Red Hen" with the class at the listening center
11:00–11:30	Make flash cards of farm animals from activity packet. Match pictures of farm animals with their names.
11:30–12:00	Practice animal flash cards with a buddy

Encourage Mainstream Students to Be Sensitive and Accepting

Mainstream students have to be sensitized about cultural differences and learn to practice acceptance and cooperation. Ultimately, we want mainstream students to accept ELLs in less structured situations, such as the lunchroom, the playground, and the school bus. Below is an activity to help your mainstream students step into the shoes of your English language learners.

➡ Ask mainstream students to pretend that they are going to live in Brazil. Tell them that they will have to go to a Brazilian school and do all their work in Portuguese. Ask your students how they would feel if they couldn't speak in class or talk to classmates. Would they be able to make friends without speaking the language? What would they do if they had a question? Do they think it would be difficult to read a science book in Portuguese or to study about Brazilian history in Portuguese?

Ask your class to brainstorm about what they can do to make newcomers feel welcome. Have them think about how they can communicate with newcomers, help them with their homework, or play together on the playground.

Another important item to keep in mind is to have a bilingual parent or student explain what a fire drill is to your newcomers. Schools in many countries do not conduct fire drills, and the noise from the alarm can be very frightening to a new student. Also, use international symbols on the bathroom doors. Some schools further help their ELLs by producing a computerized slide presentation or video to help new students familiarize themselves with the school and key personnel. A walking visit and informal introductions can also provide an effective orientation for ELLs. In the next example, Mr. Ramos pairs one of his newcomers with a buddy to help him through his first day.

➡ On the first day of school, Mr. Ramos, a 5th grade teacher, asks one of his bilingual students, José, to help Pedro, a newcomer from Mexico. José shows Pedro where the bathroom is and explains the rules for leaving the classroom. He explains what a fire drill is and where the class will go when they leave the building. He takes Pedro on a tour of the school to show him important places such as the school office, nurse's office, cafeteria, and gym. José also introduces Pedro to the principal, school secretary, and nurse.

In addition, the school office should keep a list of the people in your building who speak the languages of all ELLs. This list can include other teachers, custodians, same-language students in other classes, and bilingual parent volunteers. Make sure this list is distributed to all teachers who work with new students.

Use Classroom Buddies

Bilingual buddies can be a terrific asset for a newcomer. During the first months of school, a buddy can explain what's going on to newcomers in their native language. To ensure that your English language learners don't become overly dependent on one bilingual classmate, rotate different buddies for your student and, if possible, use classmates who don't speak the student's native language. Cross-grade tutors can be very effective; older students often enjoy teaching younger students.

You will need to teach buddies how to work with ELLs and reward students who take their job seriously. Well-organized buddy programs will help ELLs feel more comfortable in the classroom and will help the buddies gain self-esteem.

Buddies can assist new students with the classroom routine and explain specific concepts in content-area classes. They can clarify the teacher's directions and help write homework assignments. Buddies can also teach newcomers basic English such as the alphabet, numbers, body parts, classroom articles, and other vocabulary.

Friendly classmates can also help newcomers adjust socially. For elementary schools, encourage mainstream students to eat lunch with ELLs, include them in games on the playground, or sit with them on the bus. In middle and high schools, buddies should take new students to their classes until they know their way. In the next example, Won Sun and Bun Sun are paired up with buddies to help them adjust.

➡ Won Sun and Bun Sun are siblings from Korea who are new to the United States. The ESL teacher paired the boys, who were in 1st and 2nd grades, with Korean students from the 5th grade. The older students, Sarah and Hee Eun, were excited to share their knowledge with the newcomers, and they used the same teaching methods and materials that helped them learn English when they were newcomers. They planned lessons to teach during their lunch period and worked diligently to help their "students." Sarah and Hee Eun also explained the school rules and helped Won Sun and Bun Sun negotiate the new culture. The 5th grade students received a commendation from the principal for their efforts.

Sharpen Your Communication Skills

New ELLs need visual and kinesthetic support to understand what you are saying. After the first six months, they will need this support to comprehend academic content material. Use drawings, chalkboard sketches, photographs, diagrams, graphic organizers, and other visual materials to provide clues to meaning. If necessary, present your information in a variety of ways. Speak clearly and concisely at a slightly slower pace than usual. Use short, simple sentences (subject-verb-object) and high-frequency words. Your ELL students will not understand you if you speak too fast or run your words together. Pause after phrases or short sentences, not after each word. You do not want to distort the natural rhythm of your speech. Avoid using the passive voice, complex sentences, and idiomatic speech.

Involving English language learners in discussions in content-area classes can be frustrating if teachers do not develop strategies for asking questions. English language learners should be asked questions from a variety of levels of Bloom's Taxonomy. In addition to asking, "Are dragons real or make-believe?" ask students, "What makes a dragon look scary?" Expect responses that are commensurate with the student's English language level. Help students participate in class by letting them know in advance some of the questions you are going to ask. Students will then have time to prepare a response. This approach will help your students feel more secure in their content-area classes. When asking students questions, consider presenting them in the order of difficulty, as shown in this sequence:

• Ask newcomers to point to a picture to demonstrate basic knowledge such as "Point to the penguin."
• Use visual cues.
• Ask simple yes/no questions such as "Are penguins mammals?"

- Embed a response using either/or questions such as "Is a penguin a mammal or a bird?"
- Break complex questions into several steps. Simplify your vocabulary. Instead of asking, "What characteristics do mammals share?" say, "Look at the mammals. Find the bear, the dog, and the cat. How are they the same?"
- Ask simple "how" and "where" questions that can be answered with a phrase or a short sentence. "Where do penguins live?" Do not expect your ELLs to answer broad open-ended questions.

Raising your voice does not help students understand what you are saying. Speak in a quiet, reassuring voice. Show your patience through your facial expressions and body language. Speak with a newcomer individually, rather than in front of the class, when you have specific information to convey. Being in the spotlight may interfere with a student's comprehension. Don't insist that students make eye contact with you when you are speaking to them. This action is considered rude in many cultures.

Engage English language learners without making them the focus of attention with choral reading. Write key words on the chalkboard so they have visual as well as auditory input. You want them to understand what they are saying.

Because many ELLs will not understand cursive writing, be sure to print clearly and legibly. When writing notes to parents, print your message and use a pen with black or blue ink. In some cultures red is the color of death.

Check Your Students' Comprehension

Check for comprehension frequently. If you ask, "Do you understand?" you will not receive a reliable response. Many students will answer yes even when they do not understand. Your question should be more specific. Allow a response in the form of a drawing, pointing, gestures, and mime. Students can also respond using a word bank that you have provided.

Many ELLs will translate the language they hear to their native language, form an answer, and then translate that response back to English; therefore, they will need extra time when listening and speaking. Give full attention to your ELLs and make every effort to understand their attempts to communicate. Do not immediately jump in to supply words for the students or insist that they speak in complete sentences. Resist the urge to overcorrect students because too much focus on errors will make them less willing to speak. If students speak in heavily accented or grammatically incorrect English, use your reply to model the correct pronunciation and grammar. For example, if a child says, "I goed home school," reply, "Oh, you went home after school." Do not ask the student to repeat your corrected response, as this can be very embarrassing for them. Allow older ELLs to consult a bilingual dictionary, use an electronic translator, or ask for help from a same-language buddy.

If you have difficulty getting ideas across to your newcomers, ask a same-language student to interpret for you. It's good practice to keep a list of older students who can interpret in urgent situations. Keep in mind that K–2 students do not make good translators.

•   •   •

The first months are critical for ensuring that newcomers experience long-term academic success. If you want your new students to become an integral part of the school community, you need to provide them with a positive educational and social experience while they are in school (Haynes, 2005). It is important to provide newcomers with a broad, whole-district program to support their education so that they can succeed in school and fully benefit from their educational experience.

In this chapter, we reviewed strategies for working with new-comers. Your students will not always be newcomers, though. After nine months, you may notice that newcomers can partici-pate more fully in general classroom discussions and activities; however, they probably still have difficulties in content-area class-rooms. In the next chapter, we discuss the challenges that new-comers face in content-area instruction.

5

Challenges for ELLs in Content-Area Classes

Before we talk about how to help English language learners in elementary school classrooms or in middle and high school content-area classes, we need to discuss the challenges ELLs face when they are learning specific academic strategies and skills. This chapter is divided into four major subject areas: language arts including reading and writing; math; social studies; and science. The following sections are compilations of ideas gathered by the author from classroom and subject-area teachers over the past five years during workshops designed to help classroom teachers work more effectively with ELLs.

Reading Challenges for English Language Learners

English language learners will face many obstacles as they learn how to read and write in English. Because literature is culture bound, an author expects readers to share common background information. ELLs, however, are not always aware of these common ideas (Claire & Haynes, 1994). They may come from cultures where they are not encouraged to brainstorm ideas, think creatively, or express opinions. They may also be unfamiliar with drawing conclusions and analyzing characters. Story themes that are not common in a student's culture may be difficult to comprehend. In the next example, Vanna struggles with a common American custom.

➡ Vanna, a Cambodian girl in Mrs. Boucher's 1st grade class, has been in the United States for two years and speaks English fairly well. She can sound out words from grade-level material and read text along with her classmates. At the beginning of the school year, Mrs. Boucher read *What Do Fairies Do with All Those Teeth?* (Luppens, 1996) because many of her students were beginning to lose their first teeth. Before reading the book, Mrs. Boucher showed her students the cover, read the title, and asked students to predict what the tooth fairy will do with all the teeth she collects from the children. Later, she made a list of the students' ideas and asked them to draw a picture of one of their ideas. Vanna, however, was not familiar with the tooth fairy and she didn't understand what she was reading. In addition, her culture did not encourage making predictions. Mrs. Boucher can help Vanna better comprehend the story by introducing the book ahead of time and explaining more about the tooth fairy.

Classroom teachers need to help ELLs build background knowledge and teach unfamiliar vocabulary before presenting a new concept. Some specific challenges that ELLs face when reading new material include the following:

• Comprehending a text that contains a large number of unknown words. Students cannot glean meaning from context when they have too many words to decipher.

• Understanding text that includes a profusion of idioms, figurative language, imagery, and symbolism.

• Using homonyms and synonyms.

• Deciphering regional U.S. dialects.

• Grasping literary terms such as antagonist, protagonist, and denouement.

• Understanding the cultural background depicted in a literary piece.

• Recognizing correlations between letters and sounds. ELLs may come from a language background where the sound/symbol correspondence is very different from that of English.

• Comprehending the meaning of a text. ELLs will often memorize the rules for decoding written English and read fluently; however, they do not understand what they have read.

Writing Challenges for English Language Learners

Writing is one of the most difficult language skills for ELLs to master. Some of the writing challenges that ELLs face include the following:

• English language learners may restrict the content of their writing to known words and phrases. They have a limited vocabulary and are reluctant to use inventive spelling.

• ELLs often use verb tenses inaccurately. They usually write in the present tense.

• Some ELLs have not internalized the sentence structure of English grammar. This results in chaotic sentences and incorrect grammar in their written work.

• Some students are reluctant to share their work during peer editing. When they do, they prefer to work with same-language peers who may not provide appropriate feedback.

• ELLs don't have a sense of what sounds right when they read their writing aloud.

• In many cultures, students are not encouraged to express their opinions. ELLs may have little experience with creative writing in their native language.

Helping Students Avoid Translated Writing

One of the biggest challenges for teachers working with ELLs is translated writing (Haynes, 2006). English language learners will develop their ideas in their native language and then try to translate them into English. Even if students don't write down their ideas in their native language, they are thinking in their native language first. When this happens, students' writing is full of inaccurate verb tenses and unintelligible sentences. The chaotic structure and grammar that they use make the writing difficult to understand, as we can see in Duong's writing below.

➡ Duong is a 7th grade student from Vietnam who has been in the United States for three years. He is progressing well in his content-area classes; however, he has great difficulty writing in English. Despite these difficulties in expressing his thoughts in English, his parents say that he can write in Vietnamese. Duong's teacher encouraged him to write in a journal in English every night at home. He began writing in his native language and then began mixing in English. Here is an entry from his journal.

The Terrible Fight
It going to happing that three women and child were half to people. Because the fight is begin. And it going to happing that people who fight going to saw the three woman and child they saw them saw the going to flow them.

Teachers can help students avoid using translated writing by using a variety of strategies that help promote students' thinking in English. They include the following:

• Teach nonfiction reading and writing first. Through nonfiction reading, ELLs can easily access facts and language chunks that they can use in their writing.

• Spend more time helping students in the prewriting stage. Generate oral sentences and make a chart of facts about a nonfiction topic. These tools will help ELLs learn to speak the words they are going to write and strengthen the link between oral and written language.

• Help students by brainstorming vocabulary and themes with them in small groups. ELLs will have an easier time developing a subject orally in a teacher-directed small group than choosing topics on their own.

• Use graphic organizers to help students gather facts. To help beginning writers with language and structure, you can begin by creating a group web to introduce students to the idea of organizing information before they write. Create sentences for your web rather than phrases. ELLs sometimes find it difficult to rewrite their notes into comprehensible sentences. Have students practice writing from the web individually or in pairs. You can also use graphic organizer software to make a web for students to complete.

• Don't expect ELLs to edit their own work because they usually will not find their mistakes. Pick out one skill for them to edit (e.g., verb tenses) and pair them with a classmate. When you limit the text to be edited, ELLs will learn how to spot errors.

• Show ELLs models of good writing at their language level. Use mentor texts (i.e., texts that serve as a model for writing) to show a specific skill. For example, to help students write a good opening paragraph on a specific topic, have them examine opening paragraphs from books on the same subject.

Teachers should carefully consider whether to teach ELLs to use free writing and unscaffolded journal writing. During free writing, students are encouraged to write without stopping for a predetermined amount of time. The idea behind free writing is that the more students practice, the better they will write. While free writing, and unscaffolded journal writing may be helpful for some advanced students, they are not beneficial for beginning ELLs (Haynes, 2006). See how journal writing affected Rei in the next scenario.

➡ Rei is a 4th grade Japanese student. His parents are very concerned about his schoolwork and English language development. His teacher sent home a journal and asked him to write in it for 15 minutes every night. Rei finds this very difficult, so his mother writes out text for him to copy in his journal. She also completes his homework for him.

Students tend to translate their writing from their native language into English. ELLs in both ESL and bilingual programs should be encouraged to write in either English or their native language during free writing, but students should not mix the languages.

Moving Beyond Nonfiction Writing

Once students have written nonfiction pieces and you want them to move on to other types of writing, you need to carefully select the next genre. You can start by giving students real writing situations such as letters, invitations, postcards, lists, and interviews with classmates.

Encourage students to write about topics that they find interesting. Let's look at the work of Soon Sil, a 6th grade Korean student who came to the United States two years ago. Her teachers provided a lot of scaffolding during her process writing class. Here is an excerpt of her writing about a soccer game.

➡ On the day of the soccer finals, I did not want to go because the other players on my team said I wasn't good at it. My mother encouraged me to go. At the game I was sitting on the bench. Many players were injured so the coach sent me in. When there was 10 seconds left a player on my team passed me the ball and I went straight for the goal with only 3 seconds left. Then I shoot and I scored. My team won 32-31.

Math Challenges for English Language Learners

Math in a U.S. classroom may present some difficulties for ELLs, even when they have good computation skills. The language in current math textbooks can be overwhelming for students. If ELLs have low reading comprehension skills, they will struggle in math classes. Math teachers may also have challenges with ELLs who use different processes to arrive at answers, such as Gerthe does in the next example.

➡ Gerthe was a Haitian student in Mr. Burke's 6th grade math class who did not adjust well to her new environment. She failed a test on long division because she did not show her work. In her school in Haiti, students did the work in their heads and were not required to show how they arrived at the answer. Mr. Burke accused Gerthe of copying the answers from a neighbor. Gerthe was traumatized by the teacher's accusations and her adjustment to school in the United States became even more difficult.

Mental math is the norm in many countries. Students may not show their work in addition, subtraction, multiplication, and division, or they may show work in a different way than is typically taught in U.S. schools. For example, in many South American countries long division problems are written differently and work is not shown in the same way. Compare the division problems in Figure 5.1. The first example shows a division problem as typically written by a student in the United States; the second example illustrates a division problem written by a newcomer from Colombia.

FIGURE 5.1	Comparing Division Problems in the United States and South America

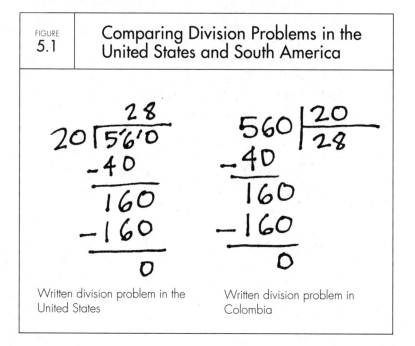

Written division problem in the United States

Written division problem in Colombia

In many cultures, math is not spirally taught (i.e., teaching a concept or skill over an extended period of time so that students learn a little more about the topic each year). For example, instead of introducing geometry in kindergarten and deepening that knowledge each year, some schools in other countries may introduce and thoroughly teach this subject in the 5th grade. Other math concepts such as estimating and rounding may not be taught as early in other cultures. Therefore, English language learners may not know about geometry for 4th grade standardized tests. In some Spanish-speaking countries, numbers are written differently than in the United States. For example, a number such as ten thousand, six hundred, and fifty-five may be written as 10.655 instead of 10,655. Figure 5.2 compares how decimals are written in the United States and in South America.

Numbers are also sometimes formed differently in other countries. For example, a "1" in many countries is written so that it resembles a "7" and a "7" has a line through the middle as shown in Figure 5.3.

Students from Central and South America can also be confused by how Americans abbreviate dates. For example, in the United States we write "2/6/06" to show February 6, 2006. In many other countries the date would be written as "6/2/06" to show the sixth day of February 2006.

FIGURE 5.2	Comparing Decimals in the United States and South America

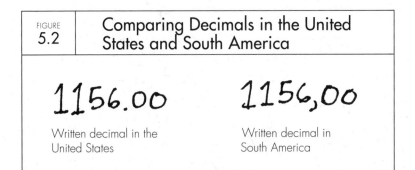

Written decimal in the United States

Written decimal in South America

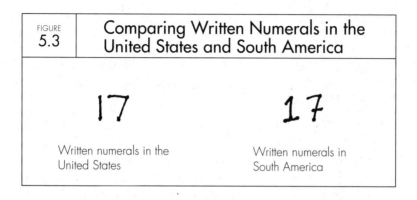

| FIGURE 5.3 | Comparing Written Numerals in the United States and South America |

17

Written numerals in the United States

17

Written numerals in South America

It is important for teachers to remember that mathematical concepts are not necessarily universal; some math concepts may not even exist in certain cultures. Math teachers also need to understand that ELLs bring other mathematics systems and their prior mathematical knowledge to their classrooms. Let's see how Ms. Meldonian helps her students understand math in a new way.

➡ In Ms. Meldonian's 3rd grade math class, students were asked to solve multiplication problems by using math manipulatives. They had to look at a problem written on the chalkboard and arrange counters in paper plates to show a specific problem. For 5 × 6 =___ student put six counters in five paper plates. Then, they had to describe how they found the answer in their math notebooks.

The English language learners in Ms. Meldonian's class who were from cultures where math facts were memorized did not like this approach. They did not pay attention during this lesson, but they wrote the correct response on their answer sheets. These ELLs had not been taught to value this process. Many of the students lacked the language skills to do the math writing.

Ms. Meldonian differentiated her instruction for the English language learners in her class and she made the students accountable for the process as well as for the correct solution. She wrote out the explanation of the problem in simple English and read it with the students. She demonstrated the explanation as students followed along using base ten blocks. Then, ELLs were asked to write and illustrate the process. After the assignment, students pasted the explanation in their math notebooks for future reference.

As shown in the example above, students from other cultures may be concerned only about getting the correct response and not about the mathematical process or justifying their answers. Math curricula in other countries could be primarily calculation at the elementary level.

As we teach more students from indigenous areas of the world, we find additional cultural differences. For example, in some cultures, people do not divide numbers; they simply subtract over and over again. Many cultures do not use fractions in the same way that we do in the United States. In the next example, Aarushi struggles with fractions in her 4th grade math class.

➡ Aarushi is a student from India who is in Mrs. Craig's 4th grade class. She is an excellent student whose math ability is far beyond that of her classmates. Although her English was limited, she easily understood the concepts taught in her math class. Because she had already been taught basic number concepts in India at a much earlier age than her American peers, it was not difficult for her to transfer her knowledge of math from Hindu to English. When the class studied fractions, however, Aarushi struggled to understand the concept. Mrs. Craig was perplexed by Aarushi's difficulty with fractions.

Mrs. Craig didn't realize that Aarushi was used to using the metric system. Instead of thinking about 3/4 of a pound of chocolate, she thinks of 750 grams. Fractions were not relevant to Aarushi at this point in her education.

Some specific challenges that ELLs face in mathematics include the following:

- Forming numbers.
- Using the U.S. measurement system.
- Using math manipulatives. Some elementary-age ELLs may not value math instruction using manipulatives. They see these lessons as "playing."
- Understanding time on a 12-hour clock. Many cultures use a 24-hour clock.

- Understanding temperatures on a Fahrenheit thermometer. Most ELLs come from countries that use a Celsius thermometer.
- Using vocabulary words and concepts for money such as *nickel, dime,* and *quarter.*

Social Studies Challenges for English Language Learners

Social studies and U.S. history classes are one of the leading academic challenges for English language learners because these students usually have very limited knowledge of U.S. history, geography, and current events. They don't have the background knowledge needed to understand the new concepts that are taught. In the next example, Ji Sook struggles with his U.S. history midterm.

➡ Ji Sook, a 10th grade student from Korea, is an advanced English language learner. He has been placed in a U.S. history class where he is having great difficulty. His teacher, Mr. King, has a very low opinion of his academic ability and thinks that he isn't really trying. Mr. King is surprised to learn that Ji Sook is doing well in his other classes.

Ji Sook has a great deal of difficulty reading his history textbook. On the last test, he memorized the vocabulary and history facts but was unable to correctly respond to the essay questions. In January, he failed his U.S. History midterm exam because he had not been able to retain the information he had memorized through rote learning.

When answering essay questions, Ji Sook was not used to expressing his personal opinion of historical events. He had difficulty drawing conclusions and making inferences unless they were directly stated in the text. One of the biggest problems for him, however, was organizing information about U.S. history. Mr. King used a time line or chronological approach to teach the history curriculum. In Ji Sook's country, history texts are organized by period.

Ji Sook's method of passing quizzes and tests is typical of English language learners. They will memorize information for a test, but because it has no relevance for them, the information is quickly forgotten. ELLs have a difficult time when they need to access this knowledge during exams or standardized tests. Even English language learners who have already exited ESL programs struggle with retaining historical facts that were not really relevant to them in the first place.

Some concepts such as privacy, democracy, citizens' rights, free will, and freedom are not directly translatable into other languages, may have different meanings, or may not even exist in other cultures. Let's take a look at how Marisol deals with the concept of privacy.

➡ Marisol is a 9th grader from San Juan, Puerto Rico. Her city is very crowded. When Marisol wants privacy, she does not remove herself physically from her surroundings; instead, she goes to another place in her mind and mentally shuts out the noise and people around her. Her American friends often intrude on her privacy because they don't understand what she is doing. When Americans want privacy, they physically remove themselves and go to a place where they can shut the door to avoid interruptions.

Other difficulties that ELLs have with history and social studies classes include the following:

- Using higher-level thinking skills for reading and writing.
- Reading text that contains complex sentences, passive voice, and multiple pronouns.
- Understanding lecture-style presentations and taking notes.
- Comprehending large blocks of text during class.
- Deciphering what is important in the text.
- Accessing background knowledge. ELLs are seldom asked to contribute an alternative view that reflects conditions in other countries.
- Understanding nationalistic or culturally focused maps. In China, for example, Asia is in the center of the map and China appears larger than on U.S. maps.

- Recognizing the proper names of countries, cities, and oceans that are not the same as students have learned in their native country.
- Understanding the passive voice in English texts. Sentence structure that includes dependent and independent clauses makes reading social studies texts very difficult for ELLs.

Science Challenges for English Language Learners

English language learners are often unfamiliar with how science is taught in the United States. Our hands-on approach may be different from what they are used to in their native countries. Making predictions and drawing conclusions independently may also be difficult for ELLs. Science vocabulary can be difficult for ELLs because it is filled with cognates (i.e., words of similar derivation or descent) and words with Latin prefixes and suffixes. This vocabulary can become even more challenging because words that students may already know in English, such as *work* or *building,* have another meaning in science.

Materials tend to be covered quickly in science classes, and science textbooks often have many concepts on one page. ELLs may find science classes difficult because in many cultures, science education is based on rote learning. Some additional challenges ELLs face when studying science include the following:

- Following multistep directions.
- Understanding visuals.
- Using science labs or equipment.
- Applying the scientific method.
- Reading science textbooks. Sentence structure can be complex and the passive voice is often used throughout texts.
- Drawing conclusions and making hypotheses during the discovery process in science lessons.

How do hands-on instruction and the discovery process help English language learners? Let's look into Mr. Corcoran's middle school science lab.

> ➡ Mr. Corcoran's students are preparing experiments for the school's annual science fair. As he preps them for their demonstrations, he explains what plants need to grow. He shows students a plant that was grown with the requisite soil, water, and light. Then, students draw a picture and label the plant in their science notebook.
>
> To help students learn how to make predictions, Mr. Corcoran presents an experiment on the effect of light on plant growth. He covers a plant with a cardboard box that has a hole in the side. Mr. Corcoran asks his students to hypothesize what they think will happen to the plant. Each day, students observe the plant and describe what happens in their science journals. At the end of the experiment, Mr. Concoran asks them to draw conclusions. The ELLs in his class, however, find it difficult to make a hypothesis. Many of these students are from cultures that value rote memory learning and do not know how to draw conclusions from that learning.

English language learners are generally able to participate in science class much sooner than they can in other content-area classes when science is taught using a hands-on inquiry method. See Chapter 6 for ideas on how to differentiate instruction in science classes.

•   •   •

In this chapter, we have seen the challenges ELLs face in reading, writing, math, science, and social studies and history. In Chapter 6, we discuss five essential classroom practices for ELLs: creating a learning environment where English language learners can flourish, differentiating instruction, encouraging flexible grouping for students in the classroom, using diversity as a resource to help all students learn, and developing alternative assessments for English language learners.

6

Differentiating Instruction for English Language Learners

What teachers do or don't do in the classroom influences the success of English language learners. Highly skilled teachers of ELLs incorporate five essential practices into their work:

- Creating a thriving learning environment.
- Differentiating instruction for English language learners.
- Encouraging flexible grouping for students.
- Using diversity as a resource.
- Developing alternative assessments for English language learners.

Creating Thriving Learning Environments

Effective teachers create a positive learning environment that lowers newcomers' anxiety level and allows them to more rapidly integrate into the classroom. Highly skilled classroom teachers have an excellent understanding of their English language learners' needs. For example, an effective teacher will immediately pair ELLs with a buddy. They will make sure new ELLs have classmates to help them, especially in social environments such as the cafeteria or the school bus. Skilled teachers provide their students with comprehensible input and know how to help ELLs access subject-area material. They tie new learning to students' background knowledge. They are careful not to water down concepts and they use simplified language for their instruction. Let's take a look at one of these thriving environments.

➡ Mrs. Pintarelli is a 3rd grade teacher with four English language learners in her class. Before a social studies lesson on comparing city and country life, she introduced the vocabulary for the city and the country using pictures. For homework, she asked the ELLs to make a list of cities in their country, to circle the cities that they had lived in or visited, and to bring in pictures of interesting sights from one of the cities.

Mrs. Pintarelli made two 6 × 6 foot squares on the classroom floor with masking tape. She invited 3 students to stand in the "country square" and 12 students to stand in the "city square." Students talked about how it felt to be in a crowded place and the advantages and disadvantages of city and country life.

Then, students were divided into small groups. One group brainstormed the advantages of city life, while another listed what is best about country living. A third group discussed the drawbacks of the city and another group listed the disadvantages of the country. Each group made a list of their ideas and illustrated them. The ELLs in Mrs. Pintarelli's class better understood the lesson because they had kinesthetic and visual experience with the concepts they were taught. They also used their prior knowledge about cities in their countries.

The four English language learners in Mrs. Pintarelli's class needed differentiated lessons that were modified to their English language ability. Notice that Mrs. Pinterelli made her lesson relevant to the experiences of her English language learners by creating an assignment about cities in their home countries. She used this homework assignment to preteach the lesson by introducing the concepts of city and country through pictures. She used the discovery process during her lesson with the masking tape squares. Students worked in small cooperative groups to generate a list of benefits and drawbacks to city living. She provided both kinesthetic and visual clues for the lesson, and ELLs had opportunities to talk with their native English peers during group work.

Differentiating Instruction for English Language Learners

Differentiating instruction may require accommodating mainstream materials for ELLs. An effective teacher's goal for English language learners is to help them gain the same knowledge as their native English-speaking peers. Repurposing materials is necessary, especially for social studies classes. Let's take a look at how the teachers in the next example revise a social studies textbook.

> ➡ Teachers at River Edge School rewrote the 5th and 6th grade social studies curriculum to differentiate instruction for their English language learners. A group of classroom and ESL teachers went through each chapter of the social studies book and picked out the most important information for ELLs to learn. They wrote a summary of each chapter, chose key vocabulary, located visual representations to go with the text, and created activities for each lesson. This work was written for both beginning and intermediate ELLs.

One lesson in the social studies textbook was about the growth of U.S. cities at the beginning of the 20th century. Here is a sample of what classroom teachers did to differentiate instruction for this lesson.

Using visuals. The teachers used many of the visuals from the original social studies textbook. For this chapter, the visuals included a map of the United States in 1900; a picture of a skyscraper; a drawing of an elevator; and photographs of Jane Addams, Hull House in Chicago, people living in a tenement, and different types of transportation, such as a cable car, an automobile, and a train. A graphic organizer was also used to visually represent the main idea.

Choosing essential vocabulary. Teachers chose important vocabulary for ELLs to learn. To present the vocabulary in context, classroom teachers used the visuals above to tell an oral story. Teachers pretaught new vocabulary in context and not through rote memorization.

Beginning ELLs were given vocabulary words with simple definitions. The students were then asked to make flash cards for the words and to study them. They also had to find the words in the beginning ESL summary section and write a sentence for each word. Their materials also included vocabulary-matching activities. Figure 6.1 shows a sample vocabulary activity from this unit using a word bank. This figure presents an excellent modification for ELLs and demonstrates how any content-area materials can be altered to include word banks.

Intermediate ELLs were given a larger number of vocabulary words and were asked to independently find a definition in the glossary or a dictionary. They also had a word-matching activity. Teachers quizzed students by simplifying the structure of questions and by substituting simpler language for some content vocabulary. For example, the sentence "What did Jane Addams do to improve life for immigrants in Chicago in the early 1900s?" became "How did Jane Addams help poor people in Chicago?"

Summarizing text. Teachers summarized the text from the social studies textbook using controlled vocabulary and simplified sentence structure. Whenever possible, the vocabulary words were defined in context. Because teachers chose the content for the summaries, the main ideas were identified and highlighted. Figure 6.2 shows a sample summary for beginning ELLs.

Both beginning and intermediate ELLs were asked to read the text and complete cloze (i.e., fill-in-the-blank) activities. The vocabulary and cloze activities were used to reinforce the material. ESL students could also listen to an audio version of the summary made by their native English-speaking classmates.

One of the benefits of this type of modification is that lessons became structured and predictable. Every social studies chapter lesson had a summary, a vocabulary page, vocabulary matching, and cloze activities. Through these independent undertakings, students were encouraged to take responsibility for their own learning.

FIGURE 6.1	Sample Vocabulary Sheet on Industries and Immigration

Word Bank

Crime	Jane Addams	Skyscrapers	20th century
Elevators	Settlement house	Tenements	Trolley cars

1. The _____ is the 100 years that begin in 1900.

2. _____ are rundown, old buildings.

3. _____ happens when people do things that are against the law.

4. _____ is a place where immigrants learn new skills.

5. _____ are very tall buildings.

6. _____ are machines that take people up and down in a building.

7. _____ are transportation that run on tracks and use electricity.

8. _____ is a woman who started settlement houses to help poor people.

Source: From *Social studies differentiation for ELLs* by S. Lautz & K. Kerns, 2005. Presentation at the River Edge School Summer Project. River Edge, NJ.

FIGURE 6.2	Sample Summary for Growth in the Cities for Beginning ELLs

At the beginning of the 20th century (the 1900s), the cities were growing very fast. Millions of people came to the cities from farms and from other countries. These are some of the problems people in the cities had:

1. The **tenements**, or apartment buildings, were overcrowded.
2. The garbage piled up. This brought rats and insects that spread disease or sickness.
3. Fire **destroyed**, or burned down, many of the new buildings because they were made of wood.
4. There was a lot of **crime** and the police could not stop it.

Many people tried to make life in the cities better. One of these people was **Jane Addams**. She started a place where people could learn **new skills** to get jobs. They could learn English. There was a kindergarten class for the children of mothers who worked. This place was called a **settlement house.**

There were good things in the new cities, too. They had parks and zoos that people could enjoy when they were not working. A new way of making tall buildings called **skyscrapers** was discovered. Electric **elevators** were **invented** that could take people up and down the skyscrapers. New forms of **transportation** such as **trolley cars** were invented to get people from one place to another.

Source: From *Social studies differentiation for ELLs* by S. Lautz & K. Kerns, 2005. Presentation at the River Edge School Summer Project. River Edge, NJ.

Using Graphic Organizers with ELLs

Graphic organizers are a powerful visual tool to further differentiate instruction and help ELLs learn content material. For example, in an assignment from the revised textbook, students were asked to complete a simple two-column graphic organizer. In the first column, students had to draw a picture or write about problems that people faced in the early 1900s. In the second column, they had to describe how the problem could be solved. The students wrote about their charts using the following phrases:

> _____was a problem in the city.
> I can solve it by _____.

They shared their charts with a small group of classmates. Through this small-group activity, ELLs had an opportunity to use oral language and review and report on what they had learned. An example of this chart is shown in Figure 6.3. Students can also complete the following activities:

• Making drawings of different examples of transportation used in the early 1900s. ELLs worked in pairs and shared their ideas.

• Learning how to sequence events in the chapter summaries by finding structure words such as "first," "second," "next," "then," and "finally." This skill helped students make more effective time lines and graphic organizers.

• Reading a short biography on Jane Addams from the library. Because the book was written on a language level for ELLs, it was easier for teachers to help students create a storyboard (i.e., a sequential depiction using drawings from the story).

Teachers can also use graphic organizers to gauge how well students learn the lesson of the day. In the preceding example, the teacher put the lesson objectives for the day on the chalkboard

FIGURE 6.3	Sample Graphic Organizer for Problems in the Cities in the 1900s

Directions: Think of four problems that the cities had in the early 1900s. Draw a picture of each problem and label it. Write or draw how you would solve the problem.

Problems in the cities	Solution to the problem
1.	
2.	
3.	
4.	

Source: From *Social studies differentiation for ELLs* by S. Lautz & K. Kerns, 2005. Presentation at the River Edge School Summer Project. River Edge, NJ.

at the start of each social studies lesson and students read the objectives aloud:

> To show the problems people faced in the growing cities.
> To show how to solve the problems.

After the lesson, the teacher asked the students to complete a graphic organizer. When students finished the graphic organizer, they were asked if the objective of the lesson was completed.

Individual teachers cannot be expected to modify content material on their own. School districts should provide teachers with professional development courses in differentiated instruction techniques and materials. The school district mentioned above worked for two summers on their material, and teachers were paid to create the lessons.

Teachers also need time to work together to share their modified lessons. Schools where teachers work together to share their expertise are able to provide an effective environment for their English language learners. If we want linguistically and culturally diverse students to gain long-term social and academic success, our school communities must be ready to provide them with a comprehensive educational program in a mainstream learning environment.

Using Think-Alouds to Help ELLs Learn

Another tool teachers can use to differentiate instruction is think-alouds. Highly effective teachers use think-alouds to help students understand the step-by-step thinking process in finding a solution. This process helps students see the strategies and the language that the teacher applies to solve a problem. Although think-alouds are generally used to help students develop reading comprehension skills, they are also powerful tools for ELLs in all content areas.

For example, in Mrs. Frechette's math class, her students understand the math concepts behind a problem, but they don't understand the thought processes needed to solve it. Let's take a look at how Mrs. Frechette models how to solve a math word problem by thinking aloud.

➡ Mrs. Frechette, a 4th grade math teacher who has ELLs in her class, restates a problem in simple English for her ELLs and asks them to look for key vocabulary to help them figure out what operation will be needed. She gives them the following example:

Apple Valley School is having a big fair. The school custodian wants to buy enough sod for the field where the fair will take place. The field is 100 feet long and 75 feet wide. How many square feet is the field that he will need to cover?

➡ Ms. Frechette demonstrates her thinking process for her students. She says, "First, does this problem make sense to me? Is there extra information that I don't need to solve the problem? I don't need to know about the fair. I can cross the first sentence out. Second, I should figure out the size and the area of the field. How will I do that? I think I will draw a picture." She marks the length of 100 feet and the width of 75 feet on the picture. "Then, I can see that I need to multiply 100×75. The answer is 7,500 square feet. Let me see, does this answer make sense?"

Encouraging Flexible Grouping for Students

Teachers should arrange the physical layout of the classroom to be conducive for small-group and paired learning. Desks should be arranged in groups of four or five so that ELLs feel that they are an integral part of the classroom community. These types of groupings give English language learners real reasons to communicate with their peers in an academic setting. Here is a conversation that occurred between Vladimir and Tommy during the lesson on cities.

> Vladimir: This is train? (pointing to the picture of a trolley car)
> Tommy: It's a trolley car. See, it runs on tracks. (pointing to the tracks)
> It runs on electricity. (pointing to electrical wires)
> Vladimir: Trolley car go on tracks.
> Tommy: The trolley car runs on tracks. It uses electricity.

Native English-speaking peers can modify their speech and adapt their oral communication to help ELLs better understand content. Small-group and paired learning provides English language learners with many opportunities for sustained dialogues with their native English-speaking peers. Students will have multiple opportunities to negotiate meaning in groups.

Teachers can also use flexible grouping to encourage choral and duet reading. ELLs can use choral reading (i.e., all students reading aloud in unison) to develop fluency and expression. This kind of reading helps ELLs develop confidence in their ability to speak and read English. Choral reading is well suited for short plays, poetry, rhymes, and dialogues. In the next example, Mrs. Palmer uses choral reading to help her ELLs.

➡ In Mrs. Palmer's 2nd grade class, almost half the students speak another language at home. Four of these students are in ESL classes and two speak limited English. The class uses choral reading to practice a teacher-made play entitled "Cookies." Mrs. Palmer sets the pace and models pronunciation and expression for reading the play. The English language learners in her class read enthusiastically.

Choral reading gives ELLs the opportunity to try out language. This practice also helps students improve their sight vocabulary and develop oral language skills. ELLs are more willing to participate because they aren't in the spotlight.

Duet reading also helps ELLs increase their reading skills. This kind of reading pairs a skilled reader with a weaker reader, such as an English language learner, to boost the weaker reader's confidence and increase his or her fluency. Skilled readers can be the classroom teacher, a parent volunteer, a cross-grade buddy, or an instructional aide. The skilled reader follows the words with his finger to reinforce the text that is being heard.

Using Diversity as a Resource

Exemplary teachers view diversity in their classrooms as a positive rather than a negative influence. You will never hear these teachers complain about having English language learners in their classes. They know that families with diverse linguistic and cultural backgrounds have unique experiences to share with classmates. They are confident that this knowledge will enrich the native English-speaking students in their class and help them learn to respect diverse cultures. These teachers make students from diverse backgrounds feel that their cultures are important, and the students are proud when their home cultures and languages are studied in the classroom. This study of the native culture is a real self-esteem builder for English language learners, such as the students in Mrs. Brush's class in the next example.

➡ Mrs. Brush adds the cultures of her students to the regular 2nd grade social studies curriculum. She chooses different cultures to study each year, depending on the students' background, and incorporates themes such as houses, holidays, folk tales, music, and games. This year, Mrs. Brush decided to study games from India, Guatemala, and Mexico. She invites the parents of her ELLs to come and demonstrate the games to her class.

The students in Mrs. Mahoney's 5th grade classroom are also learning to value diversity. By the end of the school year, Mrs. Mahoney wants her ELLs to be able to practice public speaking and related social skills.

➡ Mrs. Mahoney invited her students to share their cultural backgrounds with their classmates. Students displayed clothing, language, musical instruments, writing systems, money, food, and artifacts to their classmates. Mrs. Mahoney reminded her students how to be a good audience by reviewing what types of comments were appropriate to make at the end of each presentation. The English language learners in this class were pleased to share their culture. By the end of the school year, they felt comfortable speaking in front of the class.

Developing Alternative Assessments for English Language Learners

Because many ELLs simply memorize material for a test and don't understand what they have learned, teachers need to develop alternative assessments specifically for ELLs. These assessments should provide teachers with a realistic picture of what individual ELLs can do without focusing unduly on what they can't do.

School districts can begin by adopting a consistent grading and assessment policy for ELLs. Many schools use a pass/fail system for first-year ELLs. Other ways to create alternative assessments include increasing the amount of time given for test taking, allowing students to finish a test with an ESL teacher after school, adjusting test time for students' English language proficiency level, giving instructions in students' native language, and allowing students to use bilingual dictionaries and electronic translators. Let's take a look at the challenges that Mr. Perez runs into with his American History class.

➡ In Mr. Perez's American History class, Oscar, an ESL student from Argentina, is receiving high grades. Mr. Perez's tests come directly from a study guide that he provides to all students in his class. Students who are willing to memorize the material and give it back to him on a test receive an *A*. A few months after the unit on the U.S. Constitution was completed, Oscar's ESL teacher asked him to explain how the balance of power became a part of the U.S. Constitution. It was obvious to his ESL teacher that Oscar no longer remembered what he had memorized and that he really didn't understand the material, even though he had received an *A* on the test.

As Hamayan (1995) says, "Alternative assessments are proce-dures and techniques which can be used within the context of instruction and can be easily incorporated into the daily activities of the school or classroom." In the scenario above, an alternative assessment would have allowed Mr. Perez to ascertain how much Oscar really understood the material. An alternative assessment would have also allowed Mr. Perez to differentiate his lessons for ELLs, focus on what students know rather than what they don't know, and stress student growth rather than an absolute grade and comparisons with other students in the class.

As ELLs develop greater proficiency, teachers can modify their expectations and find more creative ways of evaluating what ELLs have learned. In the next section, we consider how to evalu-ate ELLs at different stages of development.

Assessing Beginning English Language Learners

For newcomers or students who have attended a U.S. school for one year or less, teachers can use the following activities to evaluate student learning:

• Ask beginning students to answer yes/no or either/or questions. One- or two-word responses should be accepted.

• Allow early elementary students to point to or circle the correct picture in response to the teacher's questions.

• Have students point, gesture, or act out key vocabulary and concepts from a science or social studies unit.

• Provide cloze activities using sentences from the text for student evaluation.

• Supply a word bank so that students do not have to gen-erate English vocabulary. For example, students can label a map or fill in a chart using a word bank to demonstrate their under-standing of the 13 original colonies.

- Use visuals or realia to elicit information. For example, teachers can display pictures of the jobs early English settlers had to do to survive and then ask students to discuss those jobs.
- Give students yes or no items on a list. For example, during a science lesson, allow students to signal yes or no when asked whether certain animals are mammals.
- Use hands-on tasks such as drawings, dioramas, graphs, maps, and charts to demonstrate comprehension. For a science experiment on the water cycle, allow students to demonstrate their understanding through a drawing. You can also allow students to illustrate the life cycle of a frog instead of explaining it.
- Encourage students to complete class projects in cooperative groups and grade ELLs on their participation in the group.
- Use a K-W-L chart to record student progress. Brainstorm the "What I Know" part of the chart with the whole group. Ask beginners to complete the "What I Learned" section using pictures.
- Use portfolio assessments to evaluate students' writing and oral language. Tape your ELLs' oral language on a regular basis and keep a file of their writing to measure their growth.

Assessing Advanced Beginners to Intermediate ELLs

Advanced beginners and intermediate ELLs have developed a basic vocabulary of approximately 3,000 words. Their English language ability can range from the end of the speech emergence stage to the intermediate fluency stage (see Chapter 3). There is a huge range of English language ability within these groups. Most students at this stage will be able to ask questions about the material they have studied. They will also be able to compose short stories and briefly explain concepts they have been taught. Teachers can modify their assessments for these students by using the following techniques:

- Have students role-play to show their understanding of a topic. Group ELLs with native English speakers. For example, students can act out the conditions on the Mayflower or the hardships of the first winter in Plymouth.

- Allow students to show their comprehension of a book by participating in role playing, making a cover, or designing a bookmark instead of writing a book report.

- Encourage students to complete a graphic organizer using the concept or vocabulary to be evaluated.

- Provide simplified study guides and limit assessment to key vocabulary and concepts covered in this guide.

- Allow ELLs to consult their books or notes during a test. Ask the ESL teacher to let them take open book tests in the ESL classroom.

- Allow students to answer essay questions orally.

- Have students compare and contrast concepts that were previously taught in class.

- Use a completed graphic organizer to review information in class. Have students study the organizer at home before the assessment.

- Have students fill in a modified outline, story web, chart, graph, or time line. Provide some of the answers and have students fill in what is missing.

- Reformat tests to include larger type and more white space.

- Use a dialogue journal to discuss specific topics with students. Have your ELLs respond to a particular question in the journal. For example, in a social studies class you can ask, "Would you want to be a Pilgrim? Why or why not?" Teachers answer students' responses and introduce topics in an ongoing discussion in the journals. Students can participate at their level of language proficiency.

- Simplify essay questions or break them into manageable parts. Read questions aloud and modify questions.

Assessing ELLs in Middle and High School

Some school districts require test scores and standard grades after a student has been in the United States for over a year. ELLs, however, will probably not be ready for the same assessments as their native English-speaking peers. Middle and high school teachers may be required to administer tests to help ELLs pass a specific course. If your school will not accept a pass/fail grade or an alternative assessment, other strategies to simplify tests for ELLs including the following:

• Tell ELLs in advance exactly what they are required to study for a test. Use graphic organizers, study guides, or other scaffolding to help them succeed. Include key vocabulary and important concepts.

• Simplify language and reduce the number of responses on a multiple-choice test. For example, if a question has four answers, eliminate one or two answers.

• Allow ELLs more time on a test or have students respond to a reduced number of questions.

• Highlight key words or clues on a test for ELLs. This technique works especially well for math courses.

• Provide support for essay questions by scaffolding student responses through discussion, brainstorming, and webbing.

• Allow students to use a translation dictionary during the test.

Twenty-Five Ideas for Classroom Teachers

This section is a review of all the suggestions presented in Chapters 4, 5, and 6. You may have already implemented many of these ideas in your classrooms. Consider adding at least five more into your practice, and your ELLs will certainly benefit from your improved instruction. The ideas are organized into three sections: before the lesson, during the lesson, and after the lesson.

Before the Lesson

1. Consult with the ESL teacher in your school and experiment with different activities to determine the English language learning level of your ELLs. Be realistic about what you expect your students to do.

2. Plan ahead. Look over your content to determine what concepts and vocabulary your English language learners will need help with. Think about how you will make the content comprehensible for your ELLs. As you organize your lessons, consider the following factors:

• Build on students' background knowledge. Consider showing a video or reading a book aloud about your topic.

• Remember to teach concrete vocabulary and concepts first.

• Think of creative ways to link the content of your lesson to the students' previous knowledge.

• Remember to link your current lesson with the one previously taught. For example, for a science unit on matter ask, "What did we learn about the three forms of matter yesterday? Who can name one of the forms? Today we will think of examples of each form."

• Decide what language and concepts need to be pretaught. For a major concept such as evaporation, you will need to consider how you will teach it, how you can develop content-area vocabulary, and what visuals you will need.

3. Reflect on how you can teach with oral, visual, auditory, and kinesthetic learning modalities.

4. Prepare teaching aids in advance. Assemble graphic organizers, charts, graphs, and webs for the lesson. For a unit on the water cycle, consider semantic webs or charts showing the cycle stages.

5. Add vocabulary word banks to student activities. Consult with colleagues and share your vocabulary word banks, outlines, and study guides. Remember that colleagues who work together can provide instruction that is more effective for their ELLs.

6. Adapt textbooks to paraphrase key concepts in English. Eliminate nonessential details.

7. Ask native English speakers in your class to go to the library and find nonfiction books on the lesson topic that are written on a simpler level.

During the Lesson

8. Build on what ELLs already know.

9. Use simplified vocabulary and sentence structure. Preteach key vocabulary in context.

10. Use either/or or yes/no questions; give ELLs questions in advance so that they can prepare.

11. Introduce concrete concepts and vocabulary before you move to abstract topics.

12. Teach students to categorize their information using graphic organizers. Create semantic and story maps for ELLs.

13. Demonstrate and practice highlighting techniques so that ELLs learn how to highlight important information.

14. Review and repeat important concepts and vocabulary.

15. Provide real examples and experiences.

16. Teach ELLs to find definitions for key vocabulary in the text. In science and social studies textbooks, these words are usually in bold type.

17. Help ELLs become acquainted with their textbooks (e.g., table of contents, biographical dictionary, glossary, and index).

18. Model your thinking processes for students using think-alouds.

19. Record important parts of your lesson to reinforce learning.

After the Lesson

20. Have native English-speaking classmates make copies of their notes for ELLs to use.

21. Allow ELLs to watch videos or listen to tapes about a current lesson using the closed-caption feature.

22. Provide follow-up activities that reinforce vocabulary and concepts. Include maps, charts, outlines, graphic organizers, semantic mapping, cloze activities, drawing and labeling, flashcards, games, puzzles, and time lines.

23. Encourage students to work in small groups or pairs so that their native English-speaking peers can reinforce language and specific concepts.

24. Adjust ELLs' homework assignments to their English language proficiency. Show models of what you expect on their homework responses. If you don't specify exactly what you want your students to do, either they will not do the assignment or spend an inordinate amount of time trying to complete homework that is above their language level.

25. Modify your assessments so that your ELLs have an opportunity to show what they have learned.

• • •

In this chapter, we explored the five essential practices of effective classrooms for ELLs. In Chapter 7, we discuss some of the most common programs for English language learners in the United States.

7

Programs for English Language Learners

In this chapter, we briefly examine some of the most common programs for English language learners. We saw in Chapter 2 that ELLs in bilingual immersion programs made the most substantial and enduring gains on standardized tests. In order for any bilingual program to work, however, there has to be a concentration of students from the same language background on the same grade level. Small districts may not have the population for a bilingual immersion program. However, they can still create an effective learning environment for ELLs. The descriptions here will give you a basic understanding of the types of English-only programs that are currently used in the United States.

Structured Immersion or Sheltered English Programs

In a sheltered English or structured immersion (SI) class, ELLs learn subjects such as science or history with the same grade-level objectives as their native English-speaking peers. Teachers use modeling, demonstrations, graphic organizers, adapted texts, and visual aids to clarify and enhance content-area instruction. They continually modify and negotiate the level of English used in a sheltered English class to make the content more comprehensible for students.

SI lessons are organized around language processes such as listening, speaking, reading, and writing so that ELLs can develop those skills simultaneously. In SI classrooms, teachers use modified English as the vehicle to teach content-area concepts and vocabulary. When ELLs study grade-level content in this type of setting, they have opportunities to interact with meaningful material that is relevant to their schooling.

There are several different sheltered English instruction models. Research has shown that sheltered English instruction enhances second-language acquisition and provides ELLs with meaningful uses of and interactions with their second language (Genesee, 1999).

Sheltered Instruction Observation Protocol (SIOP)

This popular research-based, sheltered instructional model was developed for the Center for Research on Education, Diversity, and Excellence (CREDE) (Echevarria, Vogt, & Short, 2004). The goal of this model is to provide comprehensible input for ELLs while helping students meet grade-level core curriculum content standards and develop their English language skills. SIOP teaching methods can be used in a sheltered English class by ESL teachers or in a mainstream class by classroom teachers. One of the most important aspects of SIOP is the intense teacher training component. SIOP training includes the following elements:

- Preparing a lesson.
- Linking new concepts to background information.
- Providing comprehensible input.
- Teaching learning strategies.
- Providing ample opportunities for small-group learning.
- Explaining important concepts.

- Providing opportunities for practicing language and concepts.
- Explicit instruction on how a lesson should be delivered.
- Assessing students in a meaningful way.

In a study comparing ELLs taught by teachers trained in SIOP with ELLs taught by teachers not trained in SIOP, students in the SIOP classes outperformed those in the control group (Echevarria & Short, 2003). Let's take a look at how SIOP is used in the next example.

➡ Mrs.Villefane, a 4th grade teacher in a structured immersion program, recently completed SIOP training. She is teaching a unit on the Pilgrims and wants her students to compare the lives of children living in the Plymouth colony in 1621 with their own lives in the present. She writes the following objective on the board: "Compare the lives of the Pilgrim children with your own lives." Next, she reexamines the chores that Pilgrim children performed by showing pictures to the class. Then she reviews a list of present-day chores that the whole class brainstormed at the beginning of the unit. Students also study unit vocabulary from a word wall. Later, students divide into pairs and each pair receives a large Venn diagram labeled "Children in 1621" and "Children in 2006." Mrs. Villefane asks the students to fill in the diagram using the lists and vocabulary posted in the classroom.

Mrs. Villefane used the skills she learned in her SIOP training to prepare her lesson in advance, link the skill of comparing to previously taught information, scaffold the activity with review, use pictures and graphic organizers, and provide students with opportunities to work in pairs.

Cognitive Academic Language Learning Approach (CALLA)

The CALLA model provides a scaffold for content-area lesson design that integrates language development with instruction in learning strategies. The language development portion of this model includes listening, speaking, reading, and writing.

Content-area instruction is based on grade-level curriculum. Students are taught the names of the learning strategies that they learn and are told why each strategy will assist their learning. Teachers present models of each learning strategy and provide opportunities for student practice. Students are shown how to transfer a strategy from one content area to another.

Chamot and colleagues (1996) reported that in classrooms where CALLA was highly implemented, ELLs performed significantly better on procedures such as problem solving than English language learners in classrooms where CALLA was not implemented. Although these findings are encouraging, CALLA researchers do acknowledge that more research and formal program evaluations are needed.

In the next example, Mrs. Leigh uses CALLA strategies to teach her class about the scientific method.

➡ After completing a unit on animals that hatch from eggs, Mrs. Leigh is teaching her CALLA science class about the scientific method. Today's lesson is on generating hypotheses. Mrs. Leigh demonstrates this lesson by showing the group a science experiment on how to tell if an egg is cooked or raw. Mrs. Leigh reviews with students what they already know about eggs. She also teaches her students the vocabulary for *cooked* and *raw* by showing them the inside of hard-boiled and raw eggs. She asks questions such as "Do the cooked and raw eggs smell the same?" "Do the whites of cooked and raw eggs look the same?" "Feel the same?" "How are the yolks different?"

Next, students are given two eggs and Mrs. Leigh asks them if they can tell which egg is cooked and which one is raw without breaking the eggs. The students use a worksheet that contains questions such as "Do the two eggs feel different?" "Do they smell different?" "Do they look different?" "If shaken, do the eggs sound different?" Mrs. Leigh asks students in each group to spin their eggs. She helps her students formulate a hypothesis and write their hypothesis on their worksheet. Students then evaluate how well they understood the lesson by writing about what they learned and what was difficult about the lesson (Haynes & O'Laughlin, 2000).

The implementation of this lesson is similar to that of SIOP; however, at the end of the lesson, students are expected to reflect about their learning.

Pullout and Collaborative ESL Programs

In English as a Second Language (ESL) programs, instruction for ELLs is entirely in English. The most popular kind of instruction in this setting is an ESL pullout. During a pullout, students are pulled out of the mainstream classroom for a minimum of 30 minutes per day, five days a week. The pullout method is mostly used in districts that have small numbers of English language learners with a variety of language backgrounds.

Another increasingly popular type of ESL support is a collaborative model. With this instructional model, ESL teachers go into mainstream classrooms to support teachers during content-area instruction. This model is most effective when ELLs in the same grade are grouped together with the same classroom teacher.

In most ESL programs, students receive little support in their native language, although some programs do have bilingual aides. ESL teachers in these programs are often monolingual.

Many school districts across the United States have a low-incidence ESL population where students of various English language levels are spread over many grade levels. These students are often grouped for ESL pullouts across grade and ability levels. To meet the needs of all the students in the ESL program, teachers may use an eclectic approach to teaching. Several ESL models are described here.

Content-Based ESL Instruction

Content-based ESL instruction is different from sheltered immersion methods of instruction. Although concepts and vocabulary from content-area subjects are used in a content-based

ESL class, the primary goal of this type of instruction is English language development using ESL methodology. Students may be pulled from their mainstream class and combined in a multigrade ESL group, or they may be taken from the same grade level and their ESL classes directly support the mainstream curriculum in a specific subject area. In both cases, students spend most of their day in a mainstream classroom.

Subject matter for units of study in a multigrade, content-based ESL class comes from language arts, science, and social studies and is often organized around thematic units. A thematic unit on the Polar regions, for example, could be taught to students in grades 2 through 4, even though this topic may be taught only to 2nd grade students in mainstream classrooms. This unit may cover animals, weather, geography, seasons, the Earth's rotation and revolution around the sun, and people living in the Arctic regions. Information and reading on a topic can be used to develop academic language. Students may also study literature or learn to do research related to a specific theme. Within each theme, teachers help students develop all four language skills: listening, speaking, reading, and writing.

The curriculum should also be aligned with the state's language arts and ESL standards. Let's take a look at how Mrs. Schnee uses content-based ESL instruction in her classroom.

➡ Mrs. Schnee's ESL class is composed of five students from three different language backgrounds. Three students are in 3rd grade and two students are in 4th grade. The students come to Mrs. Schnee's ESL class five times per week for 40 minutes. Mrs. Schnee pulls lessons from both the 3rd and 4th grade social studies curriculum. She combines listening, speaking, reading, and writing into each unit. As we look into her classroom, she is teaching map skills to her students. The goals of the group include learning the names of the continents, identifying the four hemispheres, and finding the longitude and latitude of various cities. English is taught to this group through thematic units. Many strategies from both SIOP and CALLA are incorporated into Mrs. Schnee's instruction.

Total Physical Response

Total Physical Response (TPR) is a method of language instruction developed by James Asher (2002) that ESL teachers frequently use with newcomers. With TPR, the teacher will say an action word or phrase such as "jump" or "point to your eye" and then demonstrate the action. At first, students will only be able to follow the command. Then they may also be able to repeat the teacher's words as they copy the action. The next step is to proceed to more difficult language while still keeping the instruction direct and visually stimulating. Simple TPR sequences are used to enlarge the students' vocabulary and to teach grammatical structure in context. Let's take a look inside Mrs. Clark's classroom.

➡ "Touch your head, point to your nose, and bend your knees," commands Owen as he holds up a picture of each body part. In the hallway outside Mrs. Clark's 1st grade classroom, four students can be seen jumping, hopping, turning, and touching parts of their bodies. Owen, a native-English speaker, is giving commands to the other three students, who are newcomers from Mexico. Other classmates are working in the classroom at a listening center, in an art center, or in a small group with Mrs. Clark.

Language Experience Approach

The Language Experience Approach (LEA) uses students' own vocabulary, language patterns, and background experiences to create reading texts that make reading meaningful. LEA includes the following steps:

• Teachers and students discuss the stimulus or topic for dictation.

• Students dictate the story to the teacher, who records the statements to construct the basic reading material.

• Students read the story several times with the teacher's help until the story becomes familiar. Comprehension is assured because the student is reading material that is self-generated.

• Students learn individual story words through cloze-type experiences.

• Students reinforce their reading skills through teacher-designed activities related to the story.

In the next example, Mrs. Charbonnel guides her students through a science lesson using LEA.

> ➡ The 1st grade ESL students in Mrs. Charbonnel's class gathered around a table as they watched a hermit crab crawl onto José's hand. "How does it feel?" the teacher asked. "It scratchy," José responded. Yesterday, Mrs. Charbonnel developed vocabulary and read *Is This a House for a Hermit Crab?* (McDonald, 1990). She elicited and reviewed words such as *hermit crab, shell, crawl, claw, scritch, scratch, water, sand,* and *waves.* Students dictated their ideas about hermit crabs to Mrs. Charbonnel and she wrote them down on chart paper in sentence form. When the dictation was finished, students read the story together many times as the teacher pointed to each word.
>
> The next day, the class breaks into groups and goes from one center to another. At one center, the children are listening to *Is This a House for a Hermit Crab?* on a tape recorder. At another center, students are matching vocabulary cards from the story on a chart. Other students are putting together words on colored strips of paper to make story sentences. At a writing center, students are given a sheet of construction paper with one of the sentences from the story. Mrs. Charbonnel wants her students to illustrate the sentence on a separate piece of paper. The pages will be put together to make a class book that students will take turns bringing home to read to their parents.

In LEA, students learn how to read in a second language when the reading materials are based on real-life experiences that are meaningful. Are there differences in LEA for ELLs and native English-speaking students? Although errors are regarded as an acceptable part of the process in a native English-speaking class, most ESL teachers will write the dictated sentences or words in an acceptable form. "It scratchy" would be written as "It's scratchy." ELLs are better able to recognize their own ideas and experiences in print than in the unfamiliar language of another writer.

Bilingual Programs

In this section we will look at different types of bilingual programs that show students how to learn in both their native languages and English.

Early Exit or Transitional Bilingual Programs

Transitional bilingual education (TBE) is the most common type of bilingual program in the United States. Because some ELLs fall behind in all-English classrooms, TBE is designed to increase students' academic development by providing instruction in their native language. The focus of TBE is to help ELLs develop their English language skills and to exit students into English-only classrooms as quickly as possible. Students are generally in TBE programs for three years before moving into mainstream class-rooms. For example, students who begin school in a TBE program in kindergarten are exited into a mainstream classroom at the end of 2nd grade.

Academic instruction in students' primary language will help them keep up with their classmates and will help them transfer their learning from one language to another language (Thomas & Collier, 1997). In the next example, one district considers how to integrate a TBE program for their ELLs.

➡ The TBE program in one New Jersey town is composed of self-contained bilingual classes in kindergarten through 2nd grade. The classes are taught in Spanish and Haitian Creole, and the teachers in the program have both bilingual and ESL certification. Students in each class are at different levels of English language proficiency. Teachers help ELLs develop literacy skills in their native language, and they provide students with content-area instruction in English using a sheltered instruction model. Students leave the bilingual program at the end of 2nd grade and they transition into a general education program through a pullout ESL program. After 2nd grade, these students do not receive significant native-language support. Newcomers who enter a school in this district after the 2nd grade receive bilingual language arts and math instruction as well as sheltered instruction in social studies and science.

One of the major problems with transitional bilingual programs is that many ELLs do not sufficiently develop their native-language literacy skills by the end of 2nd grade; therefore, they cannot successfully transfer their literacy skills from their primary language into English. In general, TBE programs do not meet the long-term academic needs of ELLs. Any all-English programs that teachers and administrators use as a follow-up to TBE must be designed to ensure that ELLs attain the same academic level as native English-speaking peers.

Developmental Bilingual Education Programs

Developmental Bilingual Education (DBE) programs differ from TBE programs by focusing on helping ELLs develop academic skills in both their native language and their second language instead of quickly transitioning them into English or another language. Students usually stay in a developmental bilingual program throughout elementary school, and they continue to receive instruction in their primary language even after they have become proficient in English. There are several types of DBE programs that vary by the percentage of time that students receive instruction in English. Let's take a look at how Alberto develops in the DBE program at his school.

➡ Alberto is in his fifth year in a developmental bilingual program at a school in Texas. When Alberto was in kindergarten, 10 percent of his instruction was in English and 90 percent was in Spanish. His class at that time included American-born students who spoke little English, fluent bilingual students, and newcomers from Mexico. The amount of English instruction that Alberto received was gradually increased until it reached 50 percent when he entered the 4th grade. This past school year, Alberto scored above the 50th percentile on his standardized tests in language arts and math in both English and Spanish. He will remain in the bilingual program until he enters the 6th grade.

As shown by Thomas and Collier (1997), students in developmental bilingual programs reach the 50th percentile on standardized tests in both their native language and English by the 4th or 5th grade in all subject areas. These students were able to sustain the gains that they made in English, and in some cases, to achieve even higher standardized tests scores than their native English-speaking peers as they completed high school.

To establish a DBE program, a school district needs a sizeable number of English language learners who speak the same native language. Students with various levels of English language ability can be mixed in a single class. A district also needs enough qualified teachers to continue the program through 6th grade. A DBE program also requires active support from ELLs and their families.

Dual-Language or Two-Way Bilingual Immersion Programs

Two-way immersion (TWI) programs are a growing choice for school districts that want all their students to be bilingual. Classes are composed of students who are native English speakers and students who are from other language and cultural backgrounds. The goal of this program is to provide students with bilingual language instruction and content-area instruction and to help students achieve a high level of academic achievement in both languages.

The 50/50 model is a balanced program because instructional time during the school day is divided between English and a second language (Howard & Sugarman, 2001). Because student learning in a TWI program takes place through social interaction using cooperative learning strategies, students who are already firmly established in their native language receive the best benefits from this program. The program helps students acquire a second language and develop positive cross-cultural attitudes. Let's take a look at how students operate in a dual-language program.

> ➡ Devin Clark and Maria Rodriquez are native English-speaking students who are in a 50/50 dual-language program that they entered in kindergarten. The dual-language program is a strand within their elementary school. Devin comes from a monolingual home and Maria is an English-speaking student with a Spanish-speaking father. Their 2nd grade class is composed of 11 Spanish-speaking students and 7 English-speaking students. The class also includes one native English-speaking teacher and one native Spanish-speaking teacher. The class spends the morning working in English and the afternoon working in Spanish.
>
> Students in this dual-language class study social studies, music, and math in English and science, physical education, and art in Spanish. All students in the class receive language arts instruction in their primary language. Both teachers use structured immersion models to teach content-area subjects. Because there are two teachers, students are encouraged to speak to the teachers in the language that the teachers use for instruction. Mixing the two languages and translating materials from one language to the other is discouraged. Students from both groups have opportunities to be language role models for each other during the school day.

Many dual-language programs are not 50/50 programs. Instruction in the second language may be as high as 90 percent in kindergarten, with English instruction beginning at 10 percent. As in DBE programs, English instruction will then gradually increase each year.

What Program Best Suits Your School or District?

If your school values bilingualism, a dual-language or developmental bilingual program will be the best choice. Dual-language programs provide bilingualism for both ELLs and native English-speaking students, while developmental bilingual programs strive to help English language learners become proficient in both their primary and second languages.

If your school wants a program where developing proficiency in English is the main priority, you can choose transitional bilingual programs, sheltered English programs, or ESL programs. Students are usually in transitional bilingual programs for two to three years. The long-term goal is to transition English language learners into the English mainstream class as quickly as possible. Sheltered instruction can be a free-standing program for ELLs at any grade level or in any subject area. It can also complement a bilingual program. In many areas of the country, sheltered teaching methods are being taught to classroom teachers. ESL programs are usually adopted in school districts where the ELL population is small and includes a variety of language backgrounds.

•   •   •

In this book, we have visited successful classrooms for new learners of English. We have observed how skilled teachers create a positive learning environment and provide effective instruction that supports students who are learning English. We have learned about the role that culture shock plays in how ELLs adapt to their new environment and what educators can do to ease their fears.

We have gained knowledge about the key concepts for teaching ELLs, and we have seen what research says about how long it takes students to learn English. We have reviewed the difficulties that ELLs face in content-area classrooms and learned strategies for teaching them from the first day of school. Most of all, through the scenarios, we have visited English language learners from all over the world in their classrooms in the United States.

Appendix

Activities for Professional Development Programs

This appendix describes how effective staff development is crucial for classroom teachers who are working with English language learners. A good staff development program provides educators with strategies to meet the social, educational, and affective needs of ELLs. Good programs also give teachers information about second-language acquisition, diverse cultures, and differentiating instruction for ELLs.

The 11 activities presented in the appendix can be used as a springboard for professional development programs in your school district. They are designed to help teachers and administrators meet these goals:

• Understand key concepts of second-language acquisition. The information needed to acquire this knowledge is in Chapters 1, 2, and 3 of this book. Activities 1 and 2 in the appendix review these key concepts.

• Develop cultural sensitivity and appreciation of diverse cultures in the school. Activities to raise cultural awareness are described in the appendix.

• Acquire strategies designed to help instruct ELLs in their general education classroom. Basic teaching strategies for ELLs are found in Chapters 4, 5, and 6. The information in these chapters can be the basis of an inservice program for teachers on differentiating instruction for ELLs.

The activities presented in the appendix will take approximately six hours to complete. They can be completed during two-hour sessions over three days, or at an all-day workshop, or during shorter sessions over a period of time. You may photocopy the activity sheets in this book. Before you begin, you will need to appoint several workshop leaders to be in charge of the activities; they should be familiar with the information in this book. Groups of 25 to 50 people will work well for these activities. When the groups disperse for small-group activities, make sure that the groups are small enough to allow active participation. School secretaries, custodians, and support staff should also be included in some of these activities. These tasks can be modified to meet your school's Affirmation Action inservice requirements. As you organize your sessions, remember that every activity in the appendix doesn't need to be completed and the activities don't need to be taught in the order shown.

Activity 1: What Does It Mean?

This first activity can be used as a pre- and post-test during the workshop. Have participants identify the terms that they know. Do not give them the answers when they are finished. Ask them to keep the activity sheet. They will complete it at the end of the workshop.

You may want to tailor this activity to your audience by making it harder if the faculty in your school have experience with English language learners. The answers to this activity are on page 127.

As you work with a partner, figure out how many of the following terms you can identify.

1. LEP

2. ELL

3. Bilingual

4. Comprehensible output

5. Realia

6. Culture shock

7. L1, L2

8. Proxemics

9. Dual-language programs

10. Sheltered English

Source: Adapted from "ESL Teacher as Cultural Broker," by J. Haynes, 2002, everythingESL. net. Retrieved September 26, 2006 from http://www.everythingesl.net/inservices/ crosscultural.php

Activity 2: Key Concepts in Second-Language Acquisition

There are a number of key terms that workshop participants need to know to effectively teach English language learners. These terms have been introduced in this book in Chapters 1 and 2. The material can be presented by workshop leaders in a lecture style, or participants can break into clusters of four or five people. In a group format, each group will discuss one of the concepts listed below, using this book as a resource. One participant in each cluster will be responsible for writing the key points on an overhead to share with the larger group. All the concepts will be reviewed during other parts of this professional development program so that the participants will hear these terms repeated several times. The answers to this activity are on page 128.

In your groups, discuss the following concepts:

Culture Shock

Silent Period

Comprehensible Input

Language Learning versus Language Acquisition

Affective Filter

BICS

CALP

CUP

How long does it take to learn English?

Activity 3: Myths of Second-Language Acquisition

The purpose of this activity is to dispel some of the myths and misconceptions surrounding second-language acquisition. Workshop participants will complete the exercise in pairs and discuss their responses in small groups. After the activity sheet is completed, the workshop leader should go over the correct responses orally. The answers to this quiz are on pages 128-132.

Answer each of the following statements true or false.

1. Adults learn second languages more easily than young children. **T F**

2. According to research, students in ESL-only programs, with no schooling in their native language, take 7 to 10 years to reach grade-level norms. **T F**

3. Many immigrant children have learning disabilities, not language problems. They speak English just fine, but they are still failing academically. **T F**

4. Previous generations of immigrants learned how to speak English without the special language programs that immigrant children receive now. It was "sink or swim" and they did just fine! **T F**

5. English language learners will acquire English faster if their parents speak English at home. **T F**

6. The more time students spend soaking up English in the mainstream classroom, the faster they will learn the language. **T F**

7. Once students can speak English, they are **T F**
   ready to undertake the academic tasks of the
   mainstream classroom.

8. Students from other countries should learn to **T F**
   read in their native language first because this
   helps them succeed in U.S. schools.

9. Students' culture and background will affect **T F**
   how long it will take them to acquire English.

10. Students should be strongly encouraged to **T F**
    speak English immediately.

Source: Adapted from "ESL Teacher as Cultural Broker," by J. Haynes, 2002, everythingESL. net. Retrieved September 26, 2006 from http://www.everythingesl.net/inservices/crosscultural.php

Activity 4: Yes or No?

This activity is designed to show participants how difficult it can be to alter cultural behavior. Most people don't just wake up one morning and think, "I'm going to change my cultural behavior today." Many behaviors are deeply ingrained. In the next activity, ask participants to pretend that they belong to a fictitious culture in Asia where nodding their heads no means yes and nodding their heads yes means no. Ask participants to move their heads in response to the questions below. Pause only briefly between each question.

Although the participants may intellectually comprehend that there are other ways of doing things, this understanding is often superficial. When faced with challenging situations, many people often forget the learned behavior and revert to their ingrained habits. Ask your participants, "Did you have trouble shaking your head no when you wanted to answer yes?" and vice versa. Brainstorm with the participants about some of the behaviors we expect our linguistically and culturally diverse families to adopt overnight.

1. Are you a teacher?

2. Are you a male?

3. Are you married?

4. Are you under 30?

5. Are you a vegetarian?

6. Do you work in a public elementary school?

Activity 5: The Elevator

This activity is designed to show ingrained cultural behaviors. Ask participants to visualize themselves on an elevator as they read the questions below. Participants can discuss the responses for this activity in clusters and then share their reactions with the whole group. If the group is small, workshop leaders can also outline an elevator-sized box on the floor with masking tape. Then, they can choose participants to enter the elevator one at a time. Have the audience observe where each person stands upon entering the elevator. Have the group answer the questions below.

Before you review the responses, explain the concept of proxemics to your group. (Proxemics is the study of how far people stand from each other in different situations.) The elevator activity can be repeated with groups of students or teachers from other cultures to see how the behaviors differ. The answers to this activity are on pages 133–134.

A. What are the rules for standing in the elevator? How do people stand when there are only two or three people?

B. What happens when a fourth and fifth person enter the elevator? Where do they stand?

C. How would you feel if you were one of two people in the elevator and a third person entered and stood right next to you?

D. What do people look at in a crowded elevator? How do they hold their bodies?

E. When is it permissible to talk to the other people in an elevator?

F. What would you do if someone got in the elevator and faced toward the back instead of the front?

Source: Adapted from "ESL Teacher as Cultural Broker," by J. Haynes, 2002, everythingESL. net. Retrieved September 26, 2006 from http://www.everythingesl.net/inservices/ crosscultural.php

Activity 6: What's in a Gesture?

This activity is intended to show participants that gestures are not universal. It would be very difficult for us to change our gestures, but we can be aware of those gestures that can be offensive in other cultures.

Very young students will quickly adjust to gestures used by teachers in a U.S. classroom, but older students may be offended by some of our body language. In this activity the workshop leader should model each gesture and have participants write down or discuss what they think it means. At the end of the activity, ask teachers to discuss how body language influences communication between cultures. The answers to this quiz are on pages 134–135.

Again, the purpose of this activity is to raise participants' awareness of cultural behaviors. We want teachers to appreciate the backgrounds of their students without judging them through the filter of their own culture.

1. Beckoning with the index finger, palm up and fingers curled inward.
2. Using the thumbs-up sign.
3. Pointing at something with an index finger.
4. Crossing the middle and index fingers for good luck.
5. Smiling.
6. Forming a circle with your thumb and index finger to indicate OK.
7. Waving your hand with your palm facing outward to greet someone.

Source: Adapted from "ESL Teacher as Cultural Broker," by J. Haynes, 2002, everythingESL. net. Retrieved September 26, 2006 from http://www.everythingesl.net/inservices/crosscultural.php

Activity 7: Agree or Disagree?

This activity highlights how some of our basic cultural behaviors are not universal. Many Americans have different concepts of time, space, family, and privacy. Let's examine how these concepts make us view different behaviors that we encounter in our school communities. The answers to this quiz are on pages 135–137.

After reading the statements below, decide whether you agree or disagree with the conclusions.

_____ 1. The concept of privacy is different in Puerto Rico than it is in the United States.

_____ 2. You have scheduled a conference with the parents of your Brazilian student and they show up 45 minutes late. You are annoyed and think that they do not care about how their child is doing in school.

_____ 3. Your Dominican students are always in your face. This behavior shows that they don't respect your personal space.

_____ 4. One of your Ecuadorian students teaches you a gesture from his country. You can't use this knowledge with all of your South American students.

_____ 5. Your Mexican parents keep their children out of school on the flimsiest pretexts. They don't care about their children's education.

_____ 6. Your South American students are always hugging, embracing, and touching each other. They also speak loudly and gesture frequently. This is impolite behavior in public.

_____ 7. Your new student from Argentina stares at you all the time. You decide that the student is belligerent and does not have any manners.

_____ 8. If you want your Venezuelan students to be on time for school activities, you need to clarify that it is "American" time and not "Venezuelan" time.

Source: Adapted from "Truth or Stereotype," by J. Haynes, 2005, everythingESL. net. Retrieved September 26, 2006 from http://www.everythingesl.net/downloads/ Truth2.pdf

Activity 8: State Your Point of View

This activity explores the audience's interpretation of multicultural issues and allows participants to see the continuum of cultural perceptions. You can set up a continuum by using squares of paper taped to the wall in various parts of the room. Each square should display one of the following statements:

Agree　　**Somewhat Agree**　　**Somewhat Disagree**　　**Disagree**

The signs should be displayed in the order shown above. The workshop leader will read a statement and ask participants to stand in front of the sign that best reflects their views. The signs should be far enough apart to allow room for the groups to gather, but they should be close enough to allow participants to move if they change their minds about a specific subject. Some of the sample statements are listed below.

Have the participants grouped around each sign and discuss their points of view. Then ask those participants in the "Agree" and "Somewhat Agree" groups to defend their arguments against the "Somewhat Disagree" and "Disagree" groups. Workshop leaders should not impose their views on the participants but may ask leading questions during the arguments. Encourage people to change groups if they wish. This activity gives the workshop leaders an indication of where they may need to present more information. The answers to this activity are on pages 137–138.

1. I think the United States should adopt English as the official language so that English would be the only language used by state and federal agencies.

2. My great-grandparents came to this country and no one helped them learn English. This is what today's immigrants should be doing.

3. Deep down everyone in the world is just the same.

4. When you become fluent in a foreign language, you should be able to "think like a native."

5. "We will be able to achieve a just and prosperous society only when our schools ensure that everyone commands enough shared background knowledge to be able to communicate effectively with everyone else" (Hirsh, 1987).

Source: Adapted from "State Your Point of View," by J. Haynes, 2001, everythingESL. net. Retrieved September 26, 2006 from http://www.everythingesl.net/downloads/ pointview.pdf

Activity 9: Cultural Scenarios

The following scenarios are designed to encourage workshop participants to recognize how school behaviors are influenced by culture. Have participants divide into groups of four or five members each. Hand out the list of scenarios to participants and assign each group a scenario number. Ask the groups to discuss their scenario. Then have the participants decide what the reasoning is behind the behavior in the scenario and how they would solve the problem. After this activity, you want the teachers to realize that even if they don't know what the reasons are for a particular behavior, they can find ways to solve the problem. The answers to this activity are on pages 138–144.

1. You are a 7th grade teacher with a new boy in your class from Syria. He speaks very little English. He is having a problem getting along with the other students. He has fights on the playground every day that he seems to provoke by repeatedly touching other boys.

2. You are a middle school teacher who is having a conference with the parents of an Asian student in your class. You explain to the parents that their daughter needs to spend more time doing homework. The parents keep nodding and saying *yes* as you explain your reasons. You are disappointed when there isn't any follow-up from the parents.

3. You use several cooperative learning strategies in your classroom. In the middle of the year, a new girl from South America is enrolled in your class. She doesn't follow any

of the rules that you have explained to her through a bilingual classmate, and she is very disruptive.

4. You are a 4th grade teacher and a new Korean student
    comes into your class in April. During a discussion of age
    and birthdays, this student says that she is 11 years old.
    The other students in your class are turning 10. The office
    tells you that she has been correctly placed.

5. Haitian brothers Jean-Baptiste and Jean-Pierre are often
    late for school. They are also each absent about once a
    week, but on different days.

6. You have an Argentinean English language learner in your
    class who speaks English fluently. She participates orally
    in your classroom and socializes well with her peers. She
    even translates for other students; however, she is doing
    very poorly in her content-area schoolwork.

7. You notice that a Muslim child in your class refuses to
    take a sheet of paper from a classmate. This isn't the first
    time this has occurred.

8. A child in your class hides under a bench on the play-
    ground when the town's fire whistle goes off.

9. An Asian English language learner in your class listens
    to you attentively and follows directions well; however,
    he either talks to his neighbor or daydreams when a
    classmate is speaking. He never joins in any class discus-
    sions.

10. You are a kindergarten teacher whose class is going on
    a field trip. You count your students by walking down the
    line and touching each of them on the head. You notice
    that some of your students pull back as you walk by.

11. You have an English language learner from Ecuador in your math class. He is a good student, but he becomes disruptive when you teach a math lesson using math manipulatives.

12. Your male student from the Middle East refuses to work in cooperative groups. You have tried changing the groups and putting him with a student who speaks his native language. He still seems reluctant to participate.

13. You use a red pen to write a quick note at the top of a test to the parents of one of your English language learners. The student seems very upset by the note.

14. You have a 6th grade student from China who speaks no English. He has an allergy and his nose runs constantly. He uses his fingers instead of a tissue to wipe his nose. You and your students are upset by his behavior, but he is unaware of the impact of his actions. What causes this behavior and how can you handle it?

15. A student from Eastern Europe who has learned English and can do much of the work in your classroom copies work from other students during tests. When you talk to him about this, he doesn't seem remorseful. His parents act as if you're making a big deal about nothing.

16. You are a 7th grade teacher with new students from Mexico. You suspect that they are not literate in their native language, but you wonder why they don't seem to respond to the Spanish teacher when she speaks to them.

17. A Japanese student is uncomfortable when you praise her English, and she insists that she still has a lot to learn. You try to teach her to say, "Thank you very much," in response to your compliments; however, she is even more uncomfortable. You wonder why.

18. Your new students from Africa do not seem to be able to sit still at their desks. Even though you give them frequent breaks to walk around and stretch, they are often out of their seats. What is the problem?

19. You notice that your Asian students frequently point to their noses when speaking about themselves.

20. When you speak to your student from Korea, he won't look at you. This is especially upsetting when he looks down as you are reprimanding him.

Source: Adapted from "The Culture Quiz," by J. Haynes, 2002, everythingESL.net. Retrieved September 26, 2006 from http://www.everythingesl.net/downloads/culture_questions02.pdf

Activity 10: Differentiating Instruction

Teaching strategies that help teachers differentiate instruction for English language learners cannot be learned in one or two days. This activity is designed for a separate inservice session.

Training for differentiated instruction needs to be ongoing and teachers need release time to plan and to share. Before teachers meet to prepare differentiated lessons, they should read Chapters 4, 5, and 6 of this book.

Divide participants into groups and have each group develop one of the scenarios listed below. Teachers working on the scenarios should be clustered according to the grade levels that they teach. In each group, teachers should plan an overview of a unit and write specific lesson plans for one week.

1. You are an elementary teacher who has ELLs in your class. Gather materials and make a plan of what you would need to do to successfully teach these students. Make a schedule for one week.

2. You are an elementary teacher who has several English language learners in your class. They have been in the United States for one year. Differentiate a reading lesson to meet the needs of these students. Plan activities for one week.

3. You have English language learners who have been in the United States for six months. You want to include them in your science class. For this activity, participants should divide themselves into grade-level clusters and plan a unit. Design and gather materials for one lesson from this unit.

4. You have English language learners who have been in the United States for 12 months. You want to include them in your social studies class. For this activity, participants should divide themselves into grade-level clusters and plan a unit. Design and gather materials for one lesson from this unit.

5. Your class includes a group of ELLs who have been in the United States for 18 months. Adapt a reading lesson from your classroom to meet your ELLs' needs. How can you make the material more accessible?

Activity 11: Rate Your School District

Have participants look at the following descriptions. Have them check the boxes in front of those practices that they feel their district already addresses. Ask them if there are any items on the list that their school could implement inexpensively.

☐ School secretaries or intake personnel receive training in greeting new families, minimizing students' anxiety, and understanding culture shock.

☐ Bilingual interpreters are on duty during the first weeks of school to help parents and students with registration and explain school practices.

☐ Parents are included in the school community through translated notices, school calendars, lunch menus, and other important school information.

☐ Mainstream students have been sensitized to cultural differences and practice tolerance and cooperation. Self-esteem and school morale are high.

☐ A welcome greeting and a school tour have been videotaped in various languages by volunteers. Newcomers can watch a welcome greeting and school orientation in their own language.

☐ New ELLs are placed in an age-appropriate class rather than being placed with younger children.

☐ Previously unschooled newcomers receive immediate literacy instruction beyond the allotted time for ESL instruction. ESL classes for newcomers begin on the first day of school.

☐ Classroom teachers receive some advance notice of a student's arrival so they can prepare texts, assign seating, pair the student with a buddy, and create a welcoming atmosphere.

- [ ] The school offers a half-day option for the first week for younger students to help them avoid traumatic adjustment difficulties.

- [ ] The international male and female symbols are painted or posted on bathroom doors.

- [ ] The ESL teacher's schedule includes time to support classroom teachers and train parent and student volunteers.

- [ ] Appropriate materials are available for newcomers to use in the classroom.

- [ ] A percentage of media funds is spent for books, dictionaries, easy readers, and picture books in the native languages of the student body.

- [ ] Newcomers' native language is respected and the staff encourages students to maintain and grow in their native-language literacy and cognition skills.

- [ ] School walls, decorations, and labels are welcoming and reflect the cultural diversity of the school.

- [ ] A list of all people who speak each language represented in the school is kept in the main office and nurse's suite in case of an emergency.

Source: Adapted from "How Does Your School Rate," by E. Claire and J. Haynes, 1998, everythingESL.net. Retrieved September 26, 2006 from http://www.everythingesl.net/inservices/districtcheckup.php

Answers for Activity 1: What Does It Mean?

1. **LEP** stands for limited English proficient. This term is considered pejorative by practitioners in the field. Unfortunately, it is still used in state and federal legislation.

2. **ELL** stands for English language learner. This term refers to students, not programs.

3. **Bilingual** means to know two languages. Bilingual can refer to a student who knows two languages or a program that teaches content material in two languages.

4. **Comprehensible output** refers to creating opportunities for English language learners to practice speaking English with their classmates at their level of competency.

5. **Realia** are real-life objects that are used as visuals in language instruction.

6. **Culture shock** is a normal stage that all newcomers experience. Being in a strange place and losing the power to communicate can disrupt one's world view, self-identity, thinking system, actions, and feelings.

7. **L1** refers to a student's first or home language and **L2** is the student's second language.

8. **Proxemics** is the study of spatial distances allowed between individuals in different cultures and situations.

9. **Dual-language programs** refer to settings where students from two different language backgrounds are integrated during content-area instruction. The students receive instruction in both languages.

10. **Sheltered English** is a program where content is presented in simplified English without watering down the concepts.

Answers for Activity 2: Key Concepts in Second-Language Acquisition

Culture Shock (see Chapter 1; pages 2–5)

Silent Period (see Chapter 1; pages 9–11)

Comprehensible Input (see Chapter 1; pages 5–6)

Language Acquisition versus Language Learning (see Chapter 1; pages 6–7)

Affective Filter (see Chapter 1; pages 8–9)

BICS (see Chapter 2; pages 14–15)

CALP (see Chapter 2; pages 20–21)

CUP (see Chapter 2; pages 22–23)

How long does it take to learn English? (see Chapter 2, pages 25–28)

Answers for Activity 3: Myths of Second-Language Acquisition

1. Adults learn second languages more easily than young children. **True.**

    This statement is more complex than it seems. In reviews of controlled research (Collier, 1988; Samway & McKeon, 1999) where young children have been compared with teenagers and adults, it was found that the teenagers and young adults learned a second language more readily. Children under the age of 8 outperform adults in the areas of social language and pronunciation because they usually have more occasions to interact socially. (See pages 7–8 in Chapter 1.)

2. According to research, students in ESL-only programs with no schooling in their native language take 7 to 10 years to reach grade-level norms. **True.**

In U.S. schools where all instruction is given in English, ELLs with no formal schooling in their first language take 7 to 10 years to reach the age- and grade-level norms of their native English-speaking peers (Thomas & Collier, 1997). Immigrant students who have had at least two to three years of schooling in their home country before they come to the United States take only five to seven years to reach the performance of their native English-speaking peers. This pattern exists across many student groups, regardless of the students' home language, their country of origin, their socioeconomic status, or other background variables. (See pages 25–26 in Chapter 2.)

3. Many immigrant children have learning disabilities, not language problems. They speak English just fine, but they are still failing academically. **False.**

    We often see ELLs on the playground who appear to speak English with no problem. Yet when these students are in a classroom situation, they just don't seem to grasp the concepts. Many people fail to realize that there are different kinds of language proficiency. The language that students need for face-to-face communication takes less time to master than the language needed to perform in cognitively demanding situations such as classes and lectures. It takes a child about two years to develop the ability to communicate in a second language on the playground, but it takes five to ten years to develop age-appropriate academic language. Many immigrant children have been misdiagnosed as "learning disabled," when in fact the problem is that educators assume that their social language skills (BICS) will translate into classroom performance. (See pages 20–21 in Chapter 2.)

4. Previous generations of immigrants learned how to speak English without the special language programs that immigrant

children receive now. It was "sink or swim" and they did just fine! **False.**

In a 1911 study, the U.S. Immigration Service found that 28 percent of U.S.-born students were more than a grade level behind the academic standards of the day. In contrast, 77 percent of Italian students, 60 percent of Russian students, and 51 percent of German students performed below grade level. Another factor to consider is that the level of education needed to get a job has changed. When immigrants came to the United States in the early 1900s, they could get industrial jobs with relatively little education and without speaking much English. The current job market holds little promise for those without a college education. (See ACLU Briefing Paper Number 6 on English Only at http://www.lectlaw.com.)

5. English language learners will acquire English faster if their parents speak English at home. **False.**

Research by Thomas and Collier (1997) shows that students learn English faster when their literacy skills in their native language have been developed. When parents use their native language, their speech tends to be richer and more complex. For example, if parents read a story to their child in their native language, the parents will spend more time discussing the story and answering questions. When children develop basic language concepts in their native language, they can eventually translate those skills into English. You should never instruct a parent to speak only English at home. Encourage parents to speak or read to their children in both languages if they can. Think about what you could do if the shoe were on the other foot. If you were living in Japan, would you be able to speak only Japanese to your own children after a few months? (See pages 23–24 in Chapter 2.)

6. The more time students spend soaking up English in the mainstream classroom, the faster they will learn the language. **False.**

   Children need comprehensible input to understand what is going on around them. They do not simply soak up language. For example, imagine that you are sitting in a room of Japanese speakers. You have no idea what they are talking about. You could sit there for a long time and learn very little unless someone helped make that input comprehensible. For more information, see pages 5–6 in Chapter 1.

7. Once students can speak English, they are ready to undertake the academic tasks of the mainstream classroom. **False.**

   Children can usually speak and socialize before they can use language for academic purposes. Students usually acquire BICS (Basic Interpersonal Communication Skills) first. ELLs use these social language skills to interact on the playground and in the classroom. It usually takes students one to three years to completely develop BICS. Next, children acquire CALP (Cognitive Academic Language Proficiency) skills. Students use this language for undertaking academic tasks and developing content-specific vocabulary in the mainstream classroom. It usually takes students five to ten years to develop CALP. (See pages 18–21 in Chapter 2.)

8. Students from other countries should learn to read in their native language first because this helps them succeed in U.S. schools. **True.**

   When Thomas and Collier (1997) examined large sets of data across many different research sites, they found that the most significant background variable for ELLs was the amount of formal schooling students have received in their first language.

They discovered that nonnative speakers being schooled in a second language for part or all of the school day typically do well in the early years of schooling (kindergarten through 2nd or 3rd grade), no matter what instruction they've had in their native language. But from 4th grade through middle school and high school, when the academic and cognitive demands of the curriculum increase rapidly with each succeeding year, students with little or no academic and cognitive development in their first language do less well as they move into the upper grades. (See pages 25–26 in Chapter 2.)

9. Students' culture and background affect how long it will take them to acquire English. **True.**

All students do not learn language the same way. Culture can affect how long it takes children to learn English. Do your students come from modern industrialized countries or rural agricultural societies? Do your students come from language backgrounds that use a different writing system? These factors will affect how long it takes them to learn English. Previous schooling and school expectations as well as culture shock will also affect language learning. (See pages 24–25 in Chapter 2.)

10. Students should be strongly encouraged to speak English immediately. **False.**

Many students go through a silent period. They are not ready to speak and should not be forced to do so. The silent period can last from one day to over a year. Teachers should not interpret this time period to mean that students are not learning. (See pages 9–11 in Chapter 1.)

Answers for Activity 5: The Elevator

A. What are the rules for standing in the elevator? How do people stand when there are only two or three people? If there are only two or three people in an elevator, they will usually lean against the walls, possibly in the corners.

B. What happens when a fourth and fifth person enter the elevator? Where do they stand? The fourth person usually goes to the last corner, and the fifth person stands in the middle.

C. How would you feel if you were one of two people in the elevator and a third person entered and stood right next to you? In general, you would probably feel uncomfortable. It's an accepted norm in U.S. culture that you do not invade someone's space if there is room. The general rule is that you mustn't touch each other in any way unless the elevator is crowded—and then only at the shoulders or upper arms.

D. What do people look at in a crowded elevator? How do they hold their bodies? In general, everyone turns to face the door. People will also look at the lighted floor indicator. Their hands, purses, and briefcases hang down in front of their bodies. This is generally referred to as the fig-leaf position.

E. When is it permissible to talk to the other people in an elevator? Unless all the people in the elevator are attending the same party, wedding, or professional event, strangers do not generally talk to each other on an elevator. The exception is when someone gets on with a baby.

F. **What would you do if someone got onto the elevator and faced toward the back instead of the front?** You would probably be startled and feel very uncomfortable. If you think this ritual is overstated, the next time you are on an elevator, don't face the door. Turn and face the occupants. If you really want to upset elevator occupants, give them a broad smile or wave at them.

Answers for Activity 6: What's in a Gesture?

1. **Beckoning with the index finger, palm up and fingers curled inward.** This gesture means "come here" in the United States; however, using your index finger to call someone is considered insulting in many cultures. You can expect a negative reaction when you beckon in this manner to a student from the Middle East, Portugal, Spain, Latin America, Japan, Indonesia, or Hong Kong. It is more acceptable to beckon a student by using all of your fingers with your palm facing you or by waving with your whole hand.

2. **Using the thumbs-up sign.** This gesture is considered obscene in Afghanistan, Nigeria, and Australia.

3. **Pointing at something with an index finger.** It is considered impolite to point with the index finger in the Middle and Far East. Instead, you can use an open hand or your thumb to indicate an object in the room.

4. **Crossing the middle and index fingers for good luck.** This gesture has a sexual connotation in Vietnam.

5. **Smiling.** Reasons for smiling vary from culture to culture. The Japanese may smile when they are confused or angry. In other parts of Asia, people may smile when they are embar-

rassed. People in other cultures may not smile at everyone to indicate a friendly greeting as we do in the United States. A smile may be reserved for friends. It is important not to judge students or their parents because they do not smile or because they smile at what we would consider inappropriate times.

6. **Forming a circle with your thumb and index finger to indicate OK.** Although this gesture means "OK" in the United States and in many countries around the world, there are some notable exceptions: in Brazil and Germany this gesture is obscene, in Japan this gesture means money, and in France this symbol means zero or worthless.

7. **Waving your hand with the palm facing outward to greet someone.** In Europe, waving the hand back and forth can mean *no*. To wave hello, raise the palm outward and wag the fingers in unison, however, be cautious because this gesture can be interpreted as a serious insult in Nigeria if the hand is too close to another person's face.

Answers for Activity 7: Agree or Disagree?

1. The concept of privacy is different in Puerto Rico than it is in the United States. **Agree.**

   In countries where homes are crowded, the concept of privacy is different than in the United States. In the United States, a closed door means privacy; however, in many other cultures, people go within their minds to find privacy.

2. You have scheduled a conference with the parents of your Brazilian student and they show up 45 minutes late. You are annoyed and think that they do not care about how their child is doing in school. **Disagree.**

The concept of time in most South American countries is different from time in the United States. Forty-five minutes is considered acceptable for a waiting period. If a person is too prompt, he or she is considered a status seeker.

3. Your Dominican students are always in your face. This behavior shows that they don't respect your personal space. **Disagree.**

    Although acceptable personal distance in the United States is 18 to 30 inches, personal distance in Latin American countries is much closer.

4. One of your Ecuadorian students teaches you gestures from his country. You can't use this knowledge with all of your South American students. **Agree.**

    Gestures are not necessarily the same all over Central and South America.

5. Your Mexican parents keep their children out of school on the flimsiest pretexts. They don't care about their children's education. **Disagree.**

    These families care about their child's education, but if a family member needs help, that becomes a greater priority.

6. Your South American students are always hugging, embracing, and touching each other. They also speak loudly and gesture frequently. This is impolite behavior in public. **Disagree.**

    This is not impolite behavior in South American culture, but this is part of the exuberance that defines it. Spatial concepts are different and South Americans stand much closer to each other when speaking. Norms for touching, embracing, and gesturing are vastly different from those in American culture.

7. Your new student from Argentina stares at you all the time. You decide that the student is belligerent and does not have any manners. **Disagree.**

    Although staring is considered rude in the United States, it is not considered rude in many South American cultures.

8. If you want your Venezuelan students to be on time for school activities, you need to clarify that it is "American" time, not "Venezuelan" time. **Agree.**

    Americans' view of time is very linear and being on time is valued in U.S. culture; however, in Latin American countries the concept of time is more relaxed.

Answers for Activity 8: State Your Point of View

Listed below are some thoughts on the statements listed below:

1. **I think the United States should adopt English as the official language so that English would be the only language used by state and federal agencies.** Participants need to be aware that adopting such a law would affect how people get a driver's license, access medical care, register children in school, and take the census, to name just a few important activities. The results of such a law would be far-reaching.

2. **My great-grandparents came to this country and no one helped them learn English. This is what today's immigrants should be doing.** When our grandparents and great-grandparents came to this country, they didn't need a lot of education to make a living. Many of those same grandparents never went beyond the 8th grade. Today's world is

much more complex and more education is needed in order to succeed.

3. **Deep down everyone in the world is just the same.** This statement exhibits the American perception of individualism and egalitarianism. It ignores the all-pervasive role that culture plays in human life.

4. **When you become fluent in a foreign language, you should be able to "think like a native."** This statement ignores the role that culture plays in language. It is quite common for a person to learn the mechanics of a language and speak it quite well without really understanding the culture.

5. **"We will be able to achieve a just and prosperous society only when our schools ensure that everyone commands enough shared background knowledge to be able to communicate effectively with everyone else" (Hirsch, 1987).** Just one thought: Whose background? Whose shared knowledge? This statement typically means white, European knowledge and background. It ignores the heritages of other ethnic groups in the United States.

Answers for Activity 9: Cultural Scenarios

NOTE: These responses are the author's real-life experiences with different cultures. These responses are by no means the only explanations for various cultural behaviors. The scenes attributed to students from a particular country do not refer to all members of that culture.

1. **You are a 7th grade teacher with a new boy in your class from Syria. He speaks very little English. He is having a problem getting along with the other students. He has fights on the playground every day that he seems**

to provoke by repeatedly touching other boys. American boys in grades 4 through 6 are socialized not to touch each other except during contact sports or fights. In Middle Eastern countries, boys playing on a playground often touch each other. When a Middle Eastern child does this on a playground in the United States, he will end up in many fights. The American boys may perceive this as "sissy" behavior.

2. **You are a middle school teacher who is having a conference with the parents of an Asian student in your class. You explain to the parents that their daughter needs to spend more time doing homework. The parents keep nodding and saying** *yes* **as you explain your reasons. You are disappointed when there isn't any follow-up from the parents.** In Asian cultures, nodding and saying yes does not mean agreement. It indicates that the person hears what you are saying. Many Asian parents would be too polite to disagree with the teacher.

3. **You use several cooperative learning strategies in your classroom. In the middle of the year, a new girl from South America is enrolled in your class. She doesn't follow any of the rules that you have explained through a bilingual classmate, and she is very disruptive.** This student could come from almost any culture. The organization of a cooperative learning classroom may look chaotic and undisciplined to new students because they can't tell what the rules are. This student may have come from a school where the teacher lectures and the students' roles are more passive.

4. **You are a 4th grade teacher and a new Korean student comes into your class in April. During a discussion of age and birthdays, this student says that she is 11 years old. The other students in your class are turning 10. The office tells you that she has been correctly placed.**

In most Asian cultures, everyone becomes a year older on the Lunar New Year. This holiday is celebrated in many Asian countries, including China, Korea, and Vietnam (e.g., Chinese New Year). If a child is born in September, he will turn one on the Lunar New Year in January. The student in this example is considered 11 years old in Korea but only 10 years old in the United States. This concept needs to be explained to students because it is very upsetting for an 11-year-old student to be told that he or she is only 10 years old.

5. **Haitian brothers Jean-Baptiste and Jean-Pierre are often late for school. They are also each absent about once a week, but on different days.** These students may stay home on different days of the week to take care of a younger sibling or to help their parents. The family may not have clean clothes for both children that day. Don't just assume that these students and their parents don't care about their education.

6. **You have an Argentinean English language learner in your class who speaks English fluently. She participates orally in your classroom and socializes well with her peers. She even translates for other students; however, she is doing very poorly in her content-area schoolwork.** This student has acquired BICS (Basic Interpersonal Communication Skills) but has not yet acquired CALP (Cognitive Academic Language Proficiency) skills needed to learn in content areas. Some teachers see ELLs who are able to speak with their friends on the playground and are fooled into thinking that these students are just being lazy when they are not doing their work.

7. **You notice that a Muslim child in your class refuses to take a sheet of paper from a classmate. This isn't the first time this has occurred.** If the classmate handed the paper to the student with the left hand, the child may not

accept it. In many cultures, the left hand is seen as unclean and you don't use it to hand people objects.

8. **A child in your class hides under a bench on the playground when the town's fire whistle goes off.** Children from war-torn countries may be very sensitive to town whistles for an ambulance, fire drill alarms, or even the school bells. School staff members need to be aware of how frightening such sounds may be. Fire drill alarms may cause a problem for any new student from countries where fire drills are not practiced.

9. **An Asian English language learner in your class listens to you attentively and follows directions well; however, he either talks to his neighbor or daydreams when a classmate is speaking. He never joins in any class discussions.** In many cultures, the teacher is the center of all learning. Other students are not seen as a source of information. These students need to be directly taught to listen to others, to express their own opinions, and to join class discussions. One way to do this is to have the student repeat what a classmate has said and ask the student if he or she agrees or has an opinion.

10. **You are a kindergarten teacher whose class is going on a field trip. You count your students by walking down the line and touching each of them on the head. You notice that some of them pull back as you walk by.** In Thailand, the people believe that the head is the place where a person's soul resides. In many Asian cultures, only parents and other close relatives would ever touch a child's head.

11. **You have an English language learner from Ecuador in your math class. He is a good student, but he becomes disruptive when you teach a math lesson using math manipulatives.** Students from some cultures may not be used

to working with manipulatives. Students may become disruptive because they may not take this type of lesson seriously.

12. Your male student from the Middle East refuses to work in cooperative groups. You have tried changing the groups and putting him with a student who speaks his native language. He still seems reluctant to participate. In some cultures, it is considered uncomfortable for boys to work in the same group as girls. This issue may become even more complicated if you pair a male student with a female student from his native country.

13. You use a red pen to write a quick note at the top of a test to the parents of one of your English language learners. The student seems very upset by the note. The student in this example may be upset because you have written his name with a red pen. In some cultures, red is considered the color of death, so people from those cultures don't ever write names in red ink.

14. You have a 6th grade student from China who speaks no English. He has an allergy and his nose runs constantly. He uses his fingers instead of a tissue to wipe his nose. You and your students are upset by his behavior, but he is unaware of the impact of his actions. What causes this behavior and how can you handle it? In some cultures, handkerchiefs and tissues are not used. Try giving this student a pocket pack of tissues to use in the classroom. Have someone explain to him in his language what he needs to do when his nose is running.

15. A student from Eastern Europe who has learned English and can do much of the work in your classroom copies work from other students during tests. When you talk to him about this, he doesn't seem remorseful. His parents act as if you're making a big deal about nothing.

Values about cheating are not absolute. In many countries, it is the end result that counts, not how the person got it.

16. **You are a 7th grade teacher with new students from Mexico. You suspect that they are not literate in their native language, but you wonder why they don't seem to respond to the Spanish teacher when she speaks to them.** These students from Mexico are from a rural town where a Mayan dialect is spoken. They understand little Spanish.

17. **A Japanese student is uncomfortable when you praise her English and she insists that she still has a lot to learn. You try to teach her to say, "Thank you very much," in response to your compliments; however, she is even more uncomfortable. You wonder why.** In Japan, it is considered very rude to brag about oneself. This student is uncomfortable because saying "Thank you very much" would imply that the student agrees with your assessment.

18. **Your new students from Africa do not seem to be able to sit still at their desks. Even though you give them frequent breaks to walk around and stretch, they are often out of their seats. What is the problem?** In the war-torn country of Somalia, these Somali Bantu students have never attended school. They have no experience with sitting on chairs or holding a pencil.

19. **You notice that your Asian students frequently point to their noses when speaking about themselves.** In many parts of Asia, it is believed that the soul is in the brain, not in the heart. In the United States, we generally point to the area of the heart when we are gesturing to mean "me."

20. **When you speak to your student from Korea, he won't look at you. This is especially upsetting when he looks down as you are reprimanding him.** In many cultures, it

is very rude to look someone in the eye. Young children may learn to look at adults when they are speaking, but older children will have difficulty with this behavior.

•   •   •

The purpose of these staff development activities is to help teachers and administrators understand the key concepts of second-language acquisition, acquire strategies to differentiate instruction for ELLs, and develop an appreciation of diverse cultures in the school community. Effective staff development is a key component in preparing classroom teachers and administrators to successfully meet both the academic and social needs of English language learners.

Glossary

Accommodation. Modifications to spoken or written language to make it comprehensible for English language learners.

Active vocabulary. Vocabulary words that students use when speaking or writing as opposed to receptive vocabulary, which are the words that students understand when used by others.

Adaptations. Modifications in materials and instruction made for English language learners.

Additive bilingualism. Bilingual program that promotes the development and retention of students' first language as they learn a second language.

Affective filter. Negative motivational factors in English language learners that can impede language acquisition. When a student's anxiety is high, the wall is high and language input is screened out.

Background knowledge. Also called prior knowledge, this term refers to the background experience and knowledge that students bring to classroom learning.

Basic Interpersonal Communication Skills (BICS). The language ability that English language learners need for verbal face-to-face social communication.

Bilingual. The ability to communicate in two languages.

Bilingual education. An instructional program that uses more than one language as the vehicle for instruction.

Bloom's taxonomy. Developed by Benjamin Bloom, Bloom's taxonomy is a way to classify instructional activities or questions. The lower levels require less in the way of thinking skills. As one moves up the hierarchy, the activities require higher-level thinking skills.

Cognitive Academic Language Learning Approach (CALLA). A **sheltered English** program developed by Anna Uhl Chamot and J. Michael O'Malley that allows English language learners to acquire learning strategies as well as content-area information.

Cognitive Academic Language Proficiency (CALP). The academic language of the classroom, which usually takes 5 to 10 years for English language learners to acquire.

Chunk. Several words that are usually used together in fixed expressions. An example is "Hello, how are you?"

Communicative competence. The ability to appropriately produce language both orally and in writing.

Comprehensible input. Communication that is slightly more difficult than English language learners can easily understand.

Content-based ESL instruction. An approach to second-language teaching that uses content-area subject matter to teach language. Concepts are not watered down, but the content-area language is simplified.

Cooperative learning. Students from varied backgrounds and abilities work together in small groups.

Cram school. An after-school tutoring service that emphasizes skill building through rote memorization. These schools are often run and attended by Asian students, but they are becoming more popular with native English speakers.

Culturally and linguistically diverse students. Students who are from language and culture backgrounds outside the mainstream population.

Dialogue journal. Written communication between a student and a teacher. This written conversation takes place in the student's journal on a regular basis over the period of a school semester or year.

English as a Foreign Language (EFL). A program designed to teach English to students in a non-English-speaking environment. An example is a program that teaches students to speak English in Japan.

English as a Second Language (ESL). A program designed to teach English to non-English speakers.

English Language Learners (ELLs). Students with limited English proficiency, usually students who are in an **ESL** or **bilingual** program.

English for Speakers of Other Languages (ESOL). A program of English language instruction for non-English speakers.

ESL pullout. A program where English language learners are pulled out of the mainstream classroom for English instruction.

Fossilization. An error that becomes part of an English language learner's speech pattern. This usually happens when an uncorrected error does not impede communication.

Graphic organizer. A chart or table used to organize information and ideas.

Heritage/Home/Primary Language. A student's native language.

L1. A student's first or home language.

L2. A student's second language. For a newcomer in the United States, this language is English.

Language acquisition. Picking up language through meaningful conversation that is similar to how children learn their first language. There is no formal study of forms and grammar.

Language Experience Approach (LEA). An approach to reading instruction based on information and stories developed from students' personal experiences. The stories are written down by the teacher, and the students and teacher read them together until the students associate the written form of English with the spoken form.

Language minority students. Students whose primary or home language is not English.

Learning styles. The manner in which a given student learns regardless of cultural background.

Limited English Proficient (LEP). Describes students whose English language skills are limited. Although this term is used most often in legal documents such as administrative code and law, it is considered pejorative by educators in the field of second language acquisition.

Mainstreaming. The placement of English language learners in regular education classes that are designed for native English speakers.

Mentor texts. Texts that demonstrate different writing traits of writers. Teachers can use these texts to illustrate high-quality writing to their students.

Native language. A person's first language or the language used by a student at home with family members.

Nonverbal communication. Physical communication such as gestures, facial expressions, and physical proximity that support oral communication.

Primary language. A person's first language or the language used by a student at home with family members.

Realia. Physical items that are used to teach English.

Receptive vocabulary. Vocabulary words that students understand when used by others.

Specially Designed Academic Instruction in English (SDAIE). A type of **sheltered English** instruction that allows English language learners to progress in their academic courses as they learn English. The language of instruction is adapted to learners' English level. The two major theories that are used with SDAIE are **comprehensible input** and a supportive learning environment where ELLs feel comfortable.

Sheltered English. A program in which teachers simplify the language of content-area instruction to make the content accessible for English language learners.

Sheltered Instruction Observation Protocol (SIOP). A research-based sheltered instruction model that is used to describe instructional practices that help teachers make content accessible to English language learners. Content information and language instruction are scaffolded to provide support to ELLs.

Subtractive bilingualism. A bilingual program where a second language is acquired at the expense of the first language.

Target language. The language that the learner is trying to acquire.

Teaching English as a Second Language (TESL). Teacher training programs for teachers of English language learners.

Teachers of English to Speakers of Other Languages (TESOL). The international professional organization for educators and administrators concerned with teaching English as a second or foreign language.

Total Physical Response (TPR). A teaching technique devised by James Asher that encourages language learners to respond to language with gestures and body motions. Playing "Simon Says" is an example of TPR for beginning English language learners.

Transitional Bilingual Education (TBE). A program in which content-area instruction is provided in learners' native language until students acquire enough language to participate in an English-only classroom.

Bibliography

Alanis, I. (2000). A Texas two-way bilingual program: Its effects on linguistic and academic achievement. *The Bilingual Research Journal, 24*(3), 225–248.

American Civil Liberties Union (ACLU) Briefing Paper Number 6. (1996). New York: ACLU. Retrieved May 10, 2006, from http://applij.oxfordjournals.org/cgi/content/abstract/16/3/371

Asher, J. (Ed.). (2002). *Total physical response in first year English sky*. Los Gatos, CA: Sky Oaks Productions.

Baker, C. (1998). *Encyclopedia of bilingualism and bilingual education*. Clevedon, UK: Multilingual Matters.

Baumann, J. F., Jones, L. A., & Siefer-Kessell, N. (1993, November). Using think-alouds to enhance children's comprehension monitoring abilities. *The Reading Teacher, 47*, 187–199.

Bialystok, E. (Ed.). (1991). *Language processing in bilingual children*. Cambridge, UK: Cambridge University Press.

Boehm, R., Hooone, C., McGowan, T. M., & McKinney-Browning, M. C. (2002). *Harcourt Brace Social Studies: United States*. Orlando, FL: Harcourt School Publishers.

Brush, C., & Haynes, J. (1999). Developing a multicultural curriculum. [Online article]. Retrieved September 27, 2005, from http://www.everythingESL.net

Cary, S. (2000). *Working with second language learners: Answers to teachers' top ten questions*. Portsmouth, NH: Heinemann.

Chamot, A. L., & O'Malley, J. M. (1994). *The CALLA handbook: Implementing the cognitive academic language learning approach*. White Plains, NY: Addison Wesley.

Chamot, A. U., Barnhardt, S., El-Dinary, P. B., & Robbins, J. (1999). *The learning strategies handbook*. White Plains, NY: Addison-Wesley.

Chamot, A. U., Keatley, C., Barnhardt, S., El-Dinary, P. B., Nagano, K., & Newman, C. (1996). *Learning strategies in elementary language immersion programs.* Final report submitted to Center for International Education, U.S. Department of Education. Available from ERIC Clearinghouse on Languages and Linguistics.

Claire, E., & Haynes, J. (1994). *Classroom teacher's ESL survival kit #1*. Englewood Cliffs, NJ: Prentice-Hall.

Collier, V. P. (1988). The effect of age on acquisition of a second language for school. *New Focus, 2*. Washington, DC: National Clearinghouse for Bilingual Education.

Collier, V. P. (1989). How long: A synthesis of research on academic achievement in a second language. *TESOL Quarterly, 23*, 509–531.

Collier, V. P. (1995). *Promoting academic success for ESL students: Understanding second language acquisition for school.* Elizabeth, NJ: New Jersey Teachers of English to Speakers of Other Languages-Bilingual Educators.

Cummins, J. (1980a). The cross-lingual dimensions of language proficiency: Implications for bilingual education and the optimal age issue. *TESOL Quarterly, 14*, 175–187.

Cummins, J. (1980b). The entry and exit fallacy in bilingual education. *NABE Journal, 4*(3), 25–29.

Cummins, J. (1981). The role of primary language development in promoting educational success for language minority students. In C. F. Leyba (Ed.), *Schooling and language minority students: A theoretical framework* (pp. 3–49). Sacramento, CA: California Department of Education.

Cummins, J. (1991). Interdependence of first- and second-language proficiency in bilingual children. In E. Bialystok (Ed.), *Language processing in bilingual children* (pp. 165–176). Cambridge, UK: Cambridge University Press.

Cummins, J. (1996). *Negotiating identities: Education for empowerment in a diverse society.* Los Angeles: California Association for Bilingual Education.

Cummins, J. (2000). *Language, power, and pedagogy: Bilingual children in the crossfire.* Buffalo, NY: Multilingual Matters Ltd.

Cummins, J., & Swain, M. (1986). *Bilingualism in education.* New York: Longman.

Echevarria, J., & Graves, A. (2003). *Sheltered content instruction: Teaching English language learners with diverse abilities* (2nd ed.). Boston: Allyn and Bacon.

Echevarria, J., & Short, D. (2003). *The effects of sheltered instruction on the achievement of limited English proficient students.* Retrieved August 10, 2005, from http://www.cal.org/crede/si.htm

Echevarria, J., Vogt, M., & Short, D. J. (2004). *Making content comprehensible for English language learners: The SIOP model* (2nd ed.). Boston: Allyn and Bacon.

Freeman, D. E., & Freeman, Y. S. (1994). *Between worlds: Access to second language acquisition.* Portsmouth, NH: Heinemann.

Freeman, Y. S., & Freeman, D. E. (1998). *ESL/EFL teaching: Principles for success.* Portsmouth, NH: Heinemann.

Freeman, Y. S., Freeman, D. E., & Mercuri, S. P. (2005). *Dual language essentials for teachers and administrators.* Portsmouth, NH: Heinemann.

Genesee, F. (1999). *Program alternatives for linguistically diverse students.* Santa Cruz, CA and Washington, DC: Center for Research on Education, Diversity & Excellence. Retrieved August 10, 2005, from http://www.cal.org/crede/pubs/edpractice/EPR1.pdf

Hamayan, E. V. (1995). Approaches to alternative assessment. *Annual Review of Applied Linguistics, 15*, 212–226.

Haynes, J. (1997). *Newcomer program K–2.* Englewood Cliffs, NJ: Prentice-Hall.

Haynes, J. (2002). *Science experiments with eggs*. [Online article]. Retrieved January 14, 2005, from http://www.everythingesl.net/lessons/egg_experiments.php

Haynes, J. (2004, Winter). What effective classroom teachers do. *Essential Teacher, 1*(5), 6–7.

Haynes, J. (2005, Spring). Excellent student learning. *Essential Teacher, 2*(1), 6–7.

Haynes, J. (2006, Summer). Giant steps through nonfiction writing. *Essential Teacher, 3*(2), 6–7.

Haynes, J., & Claire, E. (1995). *Classroom teacher's ESL survival kit #2*. Englewood Cliffs, NJ: Prentice-Hall.

Haynes, J., & Claire, E. (1997). *Newcomer program 3–6*. Englewood Cliffs, NJ: Prentice-Hall.

Haynes, J., & O'Loughlin, J. (2000, March) Strategies for applying content area knowledge. Workshop presented at Teachers of English to Speakers of Other Languages (TESOL) Convention, Vancouver, Canada.

Hirsch, E. D., Jr. (1987). *Cultural literacy: What every American needs to know*. Boston: Houghton Mifflin.

Howard, E. R., & Sugarman, J. (2001). *Two-way immersion programs: Features and statistics* (ERIC Digest EDO-FL-01-01). Washington, DC: ERIC Clearinghouse on Languages and Linguistics. Retrieved August 11, 2005, from http://www.cal.org/resources/digest/0101twi.html

Kindersley, A. (1997). *Children just like me: Celebrations!* New York: DK Publishers.

Krashen, S. (1981). *Second language acquisition and second language learning*. New York: Pergamon Press.

Krashen, S. (1985a). *The input hypothesis: Issues and implications*. New York: Longman.

Krashen, S. (1985b). *Language acquisition and language education*. Englewood Cliffs, NJ: Alemany Press.

Krashen, S. (1987). *Principles and practice in second language acquisition*. Englewood Cliffs, NJ: Prentice-Hall.

Krashen, S. (1988). *Second language acquisition and second language learning*. Englewood Cliffs, NJ: Prentice-Hall.

Krashen, S. D., & Terrell, T. D. (1983). *The natural approach: Language acquisition in the classroom*. Englewood Cliffs, NJ: Prentice-Hall.

Lautz, S., & Kerns, K. (2005). *Social studies differentiation for ELLs*. Presentation at the River Edge Schools Summer Project. River Edge, NJ.

Levine, D., & Adelman, M. (1993). *Beyond language: Cross-cultural communication*. Englewood Cliffs, NJ: Prentice-Hall.

Lindholm, K. (1990). Bilingual immersion education: Criteria for program development. In A. Padilla, H. Fairchild, & C. Valadez (Eds.), *Bilingual education: Issues and strategies* (pp. 91–105). Newbury Park, CA: Sage.

Luppens, M. (1996). *What do fairies do with all those teeth?* Richmond Hill, ON: Firefly Books, Ltd.

McDonald, M. (1990). *Is this a house for a hermit crab?* New York: Orchard Books.

McLaughlin, B. (1992). *Myths and misconceptions about second language learning: What every teacher needs to unlearn.* National Center for Research on Cultural Diversity and Second Language Learning. Washington, DC: Center for Applied Linguistics.

Newmann, F. M., & Wehlage, G. G. (1993). Five standards of authentic instruction. *Educational Leadership, 50,* 7, 8–12.

Oberg, K. (1960). Cultural shock: Adjustment to new cultural environments. *Practical Anthropology, 7,* 177–182.

O'Malley, J. M., & Valdez Pierce, L. (1996). *Authentic assessment for English language learners: Practical approaches for teachers.* White Plains, NY: Addison-Wesley.

Peregoy, S. F., & Boyle, O. F. (2001). *Reading, writing and learning in ESL: A resource book for K–12 teachers.* White Plains, NY: Addison-Wesley.

Pica, T., Holliday, L., Lewis, N., & Morgenthaler, L. (1989). Comprehensible output as an outcome of linguistic demands on the learner. *Studies in Second Language Acquisition, 11*(1), 63–90.

Pica, T., Lincoln-Porter, F., Paninos, D., & Linnell, J. (1996). Language learners' interaction: How does it address the input, output, and feedback needs of L2 learners? *TESOL Quarterly, 30*(1), 59–84.

Pierce, L. V., & O'Malley, J. M. (1992). *Performance and portfolio assessment for language minority students.* Washington, DC: National Clearinghouse for Bilingual Education.

Raatma, L. (2003). *Jane Addams.* Minneapolis, MN: Compass Point Books.

Reed, B., & Railsback, J. (2003). *Strategies and resources for mainstream teachers of English language learners.* Northwest Regional Educational Laboratory (NWREL). Retrieved January 7, 2005, from http://www.nwrel.org/request/2003may/textonly.html

Samway, K., & McKeon, D. (1999). *Myths and realities: Best practices for language minority students.* Portsmouth, NH: Heinemann.

Schirmer, B. R., Casbon, J., & Twiss, L. L. (1996). Innovative literacy practices for ESL learners. *The Reading Teacher, 49*(5), 412–414.

Short, D., & Echevarria, J. (2004–05). Teacher skills to support English language learners. *Educational Leadership, 62*(4), 8–13.

Short, D., Hurdec, J., & Echevarria, J. (2002) *Using the SIOP model: Professional development manual for sheltered instruction.* Washington, DC: Center for Applied Linguistics.

Short, D., & Sherris, A. (2005). *A professional development model of language and literacy for early elementary bilingual and ESL programs.* Presentation at the 2005 NABE Conference, San Antonio, TX.

Simon, C. (1998). *Jane Addams, Pioneer social worker.* New York: Children's Press.

Snow, C. E. (1990). Rationales for native language instruction: Evidence from research. In A. M. Padilla, H. H. Fairchild, & C. M. Valadez (Eds.), *Bilingual education: Issues and strategies* (pp. 60–74). Newbury Park, CA: Sage Publications.

Swain, M. (1985). Communicative competence: Some roles of comprehensible input in its development. In S. M. Gass, & C. G. Madden (Eds.), *Input in second language acquisition* (pp. 235–253). Rowley, MA: Newbury House.

Swain, M., & Lapkin, S. (1995). Problems in output and the cognitive processes they generate: A step towards second language learning. *Applied Linguistics, 16*(3), 371–391.

Teachers of English to Speakers of Other Languages (TESOL). (2006). *PreK–12 English language proficiency standards: An augmentation of the WIDA English language proficiency standards.* Retrieved September 25, 2006 from http://www.tesol.org/s_tesol/sec_document.asp?CID=1186&DID=5349

Thomas, W., & Collier, V. (1997). *School effectiveness for language minority students.* (ED436087). National Clearinghouse for Bilingual Education. Washington, DC: George Washington University Center for the Study of Language and Education.

Thomas, W., & Collier, V. (2002). *A national study of school effectiveness for language minority students' long-term academic achievement.* (Final Report: Project 1.1). Santa Cruz, CA and Washington, DC: Center for Research on Education, Diversity & Excellence.

Wilhelm, J. D. (2001, November–December). Think-alouds build reading comprehension: Help kids develop inferencing skills by using this powerful strategy. *Instructor, 111*(4), 26–28.

Index

Note: Page references for figures are indicated with an *f* after the page numbers.

About the Author

Judie Haynes has taught in elementary ESL classrooms for 26 years. For the past 20 years she has been an ESL teacher in River Edge, New Jersey. She is the author and coauthor of four books on helping classroom teachers with English language learners: *Newcomer Program Grades K–2, Newcomer Program Grades 3–6, Classroom Teacher's ESL Survival Kit #1,* and *Classroom Teacher's ESL Survival Kit #2* and coauthor of a chapter in TESOL's *Integrating Standards into Classroom Practice PreK–2.* She writes a column about elementary ESL entitled "Circle Time" for TESOL's magazine, *Essential Teacher.* Haynes is cofounder (with her son Charles) and content editor of the award-winning Web site everythingESL. net and editor of "Voices," a TESOL affiliate newsletter. She has provided professional development programs and workshops for school districts and TESOL affiliates around the United States. She has presented at TESOL's International Conference every year for the past 16 years.

Haynes has served on the National Board for Professional Teaching Standard's Committee on Standards for ESL and bilingual teachers. She is a past chair of TESOL's Elementary Interest Section and has been on the executive board of the New Jersey Teachers of English to Speakers of Other Languages and the New Jersey Bilingual Educators (NJTESOL-NJBE) for 16 years.

In 1993, Haynes received TESOL's Newberry Award for Excellence in teaching. She was New Jersey ESL Teacher of the Year in 1992. Her ESL program in River Edge was named a New Jersey Best Practice in 2002 and a New Jersey Model ESL program in 2003.

Related ASCD Resources: English Language Learners

At the time of publication, the following ASCD resources were available; for the most up-to-date information about ASCD resources, go to www.ascd.org. ASCD stock numbers are noted in parentheses.

Audio

Active Learning for Teachers: Success for English Learners by Adrienne Herrell and Michael Jordan (CD: #204249)

Be Successful with English Language Learners by John Carr (CD: #505339)

Best Practices for Powerful Learning for English Language Learners by Fay Mpras and Shirley Thomas (Audio: #204226; CD: #504360)

English Language Learners: What Do Teachers Need to Know? by Catherine Snow (CD: #505360)

Succeeding in Reading with English Language Learners by Margarita Calderon and Robert Slavin (CD: #505349)

Books

Classroom Instruction That Works with English Language Learners by Kathleen Flynn and Jane Hill (#106009)

Meeting the Needs of Second Language Learners: An Educator's Guide by Judith Lessow-Hurley (#102043)

Videos and DVDs

Maximizing Learning for English Language Learners (three 35-minute videos with a facilitator's guide) (#403326)

Raising the Literacy Achievement of English Language Learners (one DVD with a facilitator's guide) (#606122)

A Visit to a Classroom of English Language Learners (45-minute videotape with a viewer's guide) (#404447)

For more information, visit us on the World Wide Web (http://www.ascd.org), send an e-mail message to member@ascd.org, call the ASCD Service Center (1-800-933-ASCD or 703-578-9600, then press 2), send a fax to 703-575-5400, or write to Information Services, ASCD, 1703 N. Beauregard St., Alexandria, VA 22311-1714 USA.